STARTING WITH BERKELEY

Continuum's *Starting with . . .* series offers clear, concise and accessible introductions to the key thinkers in philosophy. The books explore and illuminate the roots of each philosopher's work and ideas, leading readers to a thorough understanding of the key influences and philosophical foundations from which his or her thought developed. Ideal for first-year students starting out in philosophy, the series will serve as the ideal companion to study of this fascinating subject.

Available now:

Starting with Derrida, Sean Gaston

Starting with Descartes, C. G. Prado

Starting with Nietzsche, Ullrich Haase

Starting with Rousseau, James Delaney

Forthcoming

Starting with Hegel, Craid B. Matarrese

Starting with Heidegger, Thomas Greaves

Starting with Hobbes, George Macdonald Ross

Starting with Hume, Charlotte R. Brown and William Edward Morris

Starting with Kant, Andrew Ward

Starting with Kierkegaard, Patrick Sheil

Starting with Leibniz, Lloyd Strickland

Starting with Locke, Greg Forster

Starting with Merleau-Ponty, Katherine Morris

Starting with Mill, John R. Fitzpatrick

Starting with Sartre, Gail Linsenbard

Starting with Schopenhauer, Sandra Shapshay

Starting with Wittgenstein, Chon Tejedor

STARTING WITH BERKELEY

NICK JONES

continuum

Continuum International Publishing Group
The Tower Building   80 Maiden Lane
11 York Road   Suite 704
London SE1 7NX   New York, NY 10038

www.continuumbooks.com

© Nick Jones 2009

British Library Cataloguing-in-Publication Data
A catalogue record for this book is available from the British Library.

ISBN: HB: 978-1-8470-6186-7
PB: 978-1-8470-6187-4

Library of Congress Cataloging-in-Publication Data
Jones, Nick, 1974–
Starting with Berkeley / Nick Jones.
p. cm.
Includes bibliographical references and index.
I. Berkeley, George, 1685–1753.   II. Title.
B1348.J66 2009
192—dc22
2008053026

Typeset by RefineCatch Limited, Bungay, Suffolk
Printed and bound in Great Britain by
MPG Books Ltd, Bodmin, Cornwall

To Lady Luck
(and with thanks to Dr. F)

CONTENTS

CHAPTER 1

INTRODUCTION

Father Nicolas Malebranche was born on 6 August 1638 in Paris, France. He is most famous for adapting and defending the philosophy of René Descartes, although Malebranche was also a celebrated philosopher in his own right, and indeed his own important contributions to seventeenth-century thought are often unjustly neglected.

Anyhow, Berkeley murdered him. Or rather he killed him – not intellectually, or metaphorically, but literally. At least that's what some people have claimed. According to various (typically old) biographies, George Berkeley, the Irish philosopher who denied the existence of matter, is supposed to have visited Malebranche in Paris in 1713. Word is that the two of them had such a blazing row that Malebranche's respiratory illness was badly exacerbated, causing his death two days later. In fact though, Malebranche died in 1715, some two years after the alleged meeting took place, so Berkeley didn't kill him after all. But it makes for a nice story nonetheless; just one of many nice stories that have been told about Berkeley's life, some of them true, others quite possibly pure fabrication.

Among the more dubious is the account of how Berkeley as an undergraduate wanted to find out what it felt like to be on the brink of death, and so he agreed with his friend Thomas Contarini to take turns hanging one another by the neck. Berkeley was first in the noose, but delayed giving the pre-arranged signal to be let down, promptly passed out, and on regaining consciousness complained that his shirt collar was creased. ("Bless my heart, Contarini, you have rumpled my band", he reportedly exclaimed.)

Indeed it was claimed in the very first biographical summary of Berkeley's life, and probably outrageously, that he was generally considered something of a buffoon and a figure of fun at University. One of the more famous jokes allegedly told at his expense involved Berkeley the immaterialist variously smacking his head or being hit with a stick or some such, only for a top wit looking on to quip with delight that it was 'no matter'.

Berkeley also came up with a plan to build a college on the island of Bermuda (some six hundred miles away from the nearest mainland), proposed that the sons of indigenous Indians might be kidnapped from America to help populate the college, championed 'tar water' as a cure for all ills, controversially refused to wear any powder in his wig so long as the Irish poor relied on flour to avoid starvation, and looked after Cornelius the Giant for a month in 1752.

In short, some people in the past have come all too easily to the careless and wrong-headed view that George Berkeley the man was a bit of a dunce. And so too, it's all too easy for students today coming to Berkeley for the first time to get the impression that his philosophical views are similarly ridiculous. After all, he is the philosopher who claimed that there are no such things as material objects, that tables and chairs are nothing more than collections of ideas in our minds, that minds and ideas are the only things that exist, and that God neatly coordinates the sensory experiences we each have in such a way that we are all partaking in the same 'virtual reality', as we might say today. It might be thought that these claims are nothing more than a lightweight and indefensible fantasy, and that Berkeley's philosophical beliefs, far from being something that we should take seriously, are so far removed from our own ways of thinking about the world that they should be dismissed out of hand as quackery, and the quackery of a long-dead Irishman at that.

Most philosophy teachers today don't hold this view, thankfully. Yet some of them do still think that Berkeley's reasoning can be *easily* rebutted, and that studying his arguments is useful only insofar as doing so provides novice students with an opportunity to sharpen their fledgling analytical skills on some fairly disposable cannon fodder. In this book I am going to try to persuade you that Berkeley's philosophical arguments for his crazy-sounding conclusions are in fact more sophisticated than are often thought, and can't be defeated as easily as is commonly supposed. But before I even think about doing that, there are some preliminaries that should be attended to so that we will be in a good position in due course to start examining and thinking about what Berkeley had to say. In the remainder of this Introduction, I'm going to provide another brief, though hopefully more rounded, biographical sketch of the key stages in Berkeley's life, before giving an overview of his major written works and their interrelation, and finishing off with some guidelines for how you should go about engaging with a philosopher like Berkeley. Of course, if you're not too interested in all that, you can simply skip to Chapter 2 (if you want to read about Berkeley's place in the philosophical tradition, and the philosophers and theories that influenced his own views), or Chapter 3 (if you really want to cut straight to the chase and engage with Berkeley's philosophy itself).

i. AN OVERVIEW OF BERKELEY'S LIFE

George Berkeley was born near Kilkenny (approximately seventy miles south-west of Dublin) in Ireland on 12 March 1685, and he died aged 67 on 14 January 1753 in Oxford, England. He was apparently the eldest of six sons to his parents, William (who had emigrated from England, and was a man of some standing and financial means) and Elisabeth. Having grown up in (or in the grounds of) Dysart Castle, ten miles or so from Kilkenny, Berkeley went to school at Kilkenny College (sometimes nicknamed 'the Eton of Ireland') and to university at Trinity College, Dublin. After completing his BA degree in 1704, aged 18, he secured a position as a Fellow (roughly, a member of academic staff) at Trinity in 1707, which required him to be ordained in the Anglican Church. Having secured a postgraduate degree in 1707, and written his three most famous philosophical works (the *New Theory of Vision*, the

Principles and the *Dialogues*) at Trinity by the age of 28, he moved to London in 1713 and started moving in the circles of royalty and the literati. (Among other people, he was friends with Jonathan Swift (of *Gulliver's Travels* fame) and the poet Alexander Pope.)

Over the next eight years, he undertook two trips to Continental Europe. The first of these, from 1713 to 1714, saw him travel to France in the capacity of chaplain to the Earl of Peterborough (who was due to attend the coronation of the King of Sicily), before spending some time in Italy. The second, from 1716 to 1720, took the form of a Grand Tour, with Berkeley acting this time as the tutor to the teenage son of an Irish bishop, again with stays in Italy and the then republic of Venice taking up much of his time. On his return to London after each trip he continued where he left off, cementing his place in high society and aiming to secure a Preferment (a fancy job, bestowed by the monarch).

In 1721, still waiting for that top job, he returned to Trinity, Dublin, to become actively involved in academic life as a Senior Fellow until 1724, when he was installed as the Dean of Derry (in the north of what is now Northern Ireland). This was a post he would hold, albeit only in name, for just under ten years. Instead of residing in Derry he palmed off his duties to someone else and returned to London from 1724 to 1728 to generate support for his 'Bermuda Project'. Berkeley felt called by God to establish a college on the island of Bermuda to educate and train for missionary work both native American Indians, and the sons of immigrant Englishmen working on American plantations. In 1728 (having married Anne Forster, the daughter of a former Speaker of the Irish House of Commons, earlier that year) he moved to Newport, Rhode Island, in America to further plan the Bermuda Project. (He had been promised a grant by the British government before he left London, and had also secured many private pledges of support and funding.)

For much of the time in America, Berkeley could only sit and wait for the promised government grant to materialize. He was far from idle though – among other things he wrote another book (his *Alciphron*), fathered two children, preached in local churches, and helped further the causes of the early American universities at Harvard and Yale. (And on an American note, what is now the city of Berkeley, California would be named after him in the nineteenth century, after one of the members of the College of California recalled the opening line to a poem Berkeley had written when envisioning his Bermuda Project – "Westward the course of empire takes its way".)

Berkeley returned to England in 1731, once it became clear that the funds he had been promised by the British government were not going to materialize, and he was forced, reluctantly, to abandon the Project. Rejoining London high society, he waited to be given another top job, which transpired in 1734 when he was appointed Bishop of Cloyne back in Ireland. (Cloyne itself is about ten miles to the east of the city of Cork, near the southern coast of Ireland.) Berkeley did take up his ecclesiastical duties this time, and indeed he was very much a 'hands-on' bishop, with a deep concern for the welfare of the poor in his diocese, and for the economic and political plight of Ireland in general. Among other things, for example, he set up a farm (which his wife ran) which provided employment for more than a hundred workers, controversially encouraged the wealthy to wear homespun clothing (rather than more fashionable imports), provided charity during times of poverty, and tended to the sick himself in the absence of local physicians. It was during this time that he championed the use of 'tar water', a solution made from a vegetable extract from tree bark, as a cure-all. Berkeley's book *Siris*, which he published while at Cloyne, contained an analysis of the chemical properties of tar water, along with instructions for its production. Notably, drinking tar water as a tonic became very fashionable as a result of this book, even making its way into respectable medical books for many years to come as something that it wouldn't do you any harm to take.

He remained at Cloyne until 1752, when he moved back to England, installing himself and his family at Oxford so that he could oversee his son George's university education. (His son had pretty expensive tastes it would seem, but then again, keeping horses and employing servants tended to be a costly business. It appears that dad was happy enough to foot the bill.) Berkeley died peacefully in Oxford the following year, reportedly while listening to and commenting on a passage from the Bible that his daughter was reading out to the family. In accordance with his will, once a sufficient number of days had passed to ensure that he really was dead, he was buried in the parish in which he died, in the chapel of Christ Church College, Oxford. Over the course of his life he fathered seven children, three of whom died in infancy. Another (William, of whom Berkeley was particularly fond) died before reaching adulthood, and only one of them (George) went on to have children of his own.

ii. BERKELEY'S WORKS AND HOW THEY INTERRELATE

Berkeley had written some of the most important books in the history of philosophy before he hit 30, books which would significantly influence the evolution of philosophical thinking in the Western world, and which are still (in some cases widely) read today.

His *magnum opus*, *A Treatise concerning the Principles of Human Knowledge*, appeared in 1710 when Berkeley was just 25 years old. By this time he had already produced a pioneering work on the philosophy of sense perception the previous year, his *Essay toward a New Theory of Vision*. And in 1713, when he was 28, he published his most accessible book, and arguably his finest piece of literature, *Three Dialogues between Hylas and Philonous*.

A Treatise concerning the Principles of Human Knowledge and *Three Dialogues between Hylas and Philonous* are by far and a way the most important resources for people wanting to study Berkeley's philosophy, and their contents will be our main focus in *Starting with Berkeley*. I will say something in a moment about these two books and their interrelation. Just before I do though, you should be aware that Berkeley wasn't just a philosopher – he was a polymath. He had his fingers in all manner of pies during his lifetime, and he had an interest and often expertise in many subjects related to philosophy and beyond philosophy; for example in mathematics, theology, economics and science. This is reflected by the fact that Berkeley wrote essays, pamphlets and books on many topics, and I will a say little something in due course about the other main writings he produced in his lifetime and their relation to his two major philosophical works.

A Treatise Concerning the Principles of Human Knowledge (1710)

This book is the fullest and most scholarly expression of Berkeley's philosophy that he wrote. Today it's more often referred to as the *Principles of Human Knowledge*, and most often simply as the *Principles*. In it, Berkeley lays out in detail his reasons for rejecting many of the prevailing philosophical doctrines of the day, and presents his own, positive theories chiefly concerning *epistemology* (to do with what we can know, and how we can know it) and *metaphysics* (to do with the ultimate nature of reality).

In fact, the main body of the *Principles* is labelled as 'Part I' by Berkeley, and he records or implies in his letters and his notebooks that he originally intended to write further Parts, dealing in far more detail with topics he only just touched on, if at all, in Part I. For example, in 1729 he writes in a letter to his friend Samuel Johnson (N.B., not the famous dictionary-writing Dr. Samuel Johnson) that he had lost the manuscript for Part II when travelling in Italy some years before. What has survived to this day, in addition to Part I, is a general introduction to all the intended Parts of the *Principles*, which was originally and still is published in conjunction with Part I. In what is commonly called the 'Introduction to the *Principles*', Berkeley makes his preparations for his attack on his philosophical opponents' theories, and for his defence of his own philosophy. He does so by identifying what he takes to be some fundamental mistakes concerning the ways words are taken to work, and the kinds of ideas they are taken to stand for. Crucially here he introduces his famous attack on 'abstract ideas', which we will be looking at in detail in Chapter 4.

Having published the first edition of the *Principles* in 1710, Berkeley was dismayed to find that it wasn't well received. Indeed it was typically ridiculed and/or ignored by those people he personally made copies available to, and it certainly didn't provoke any published controversy or debate at the time, still less any public converts to Berkeley's philosophical views. His own opinion was that this was down at least in part to the fact that the *Principles* was published in Dublin, which would have restricted its availability, and the fact that he had cast the book in terms suitable for an academic audience who were familiar with the technical vocabulary employed by the philosophers and scientists of the day. It was only after the better reception afforded to his *Alciphron*, the book that enjoyed the most success during his lifetime, that Berkeley published a second edition of the *Principles*, with a handful of minor amendments, in 1734.

Three Dialogues between Hylas and Philonous (1713)

It was the reaction, or rather lack of it, to the *Principles* that prompted Berkeley to write his *Three Dialogues between Hylas and Philonous* (or simply the *Dialogues*, as it is often called today). It was published three years after the *Principles*, in London this time, and it is Berkeley's attempt to make his philosophy more accessible and available to a far wider audience. Gone is much of the technical language of the *Principles*, and instead of straightforward prose the book takes the form of a conversation between the two characters in the title – at first glance the book looks very much like a play script. This dialogue form was famously employed by the ancient Greek philosopher Plato, whom Berkeley very much admired, and with the *Dialogues* we have not just a philosophical work, but also possibly the most elegant and well-constructed piece of literature in this form since Plato's day.

The conversation between Hylas and Philonous is portrayed as taking place over three days, in the setting of a garden in the grounds of a college or university, with the three days corresponding to the First, Second and Third Dialogue which make up the book. Philonous, whose name means 'lover of mind' in ancient Greek, is Berkeley's mouthpiece, roughly speaking, while Hylas, whose name derives from the ancient Greek word for 'matter', is Berkeley's stooge, again roughly speaking. (I say roughly speaking in each case because there is some debate between academics about the precise extent to which Philonous' views are those of Berkeley, and to which Hylas' views are those to which Berkeley was opposed. For our purposes though, this characterization is certainly accurate enough.) While it's never made explicitly clear, the relationship between Hylas and Philonous seems to be that between, respectively, a more junior and a more senior member of the university or college.

At the start of the *Dialogues*, Hylas is astonished to hear that Philonous denies that there is any such thing as matter in existence, and over the course of their conversation, Philonous gradually persuades him that this is in fact the case. Philonous presents Hylas with arguments, many of which are familiar from the *Principles*, and responds to the many and varied objections which Hylas comes up with. By the end of the book, Hylas has conceded each of Philonous' points, even though it is quite amusing on occasion just how quickly he does so. (On other occasions though Hylas is far more tenacious and takes a great deal of persuading.)

In terms of its philosophical content, the *Dialogues* repeats many, though by no means all, of Berkeley's arguments from the *Principles*. There is no substantial change of doctrine between the two books, so that together they present a unified body of work, although certain arguments and points are given more or less emphasis in one book or the other, and as well as the omissions there are also some new arguments in the *Dialogues*. Overall, while the *Principles* for most people's money remains the most important expression of Berkeley's philosophical beliefs, the *Dialogues* supplements the *Principles* nicely, and there is some material in the *Dialogues* that helps to clarify, or indeed strengthens, the positions he adopts in the *Principles*. It is also the case that the *Dialogues* is a joy to read, more so than the *Principles*, as you will hopefully find out for yourself.

It appears that despite Berkeley's best intentions, the *Dialogues* was barely any more successful on its first publication than the *Principles* had been. Having said this, a second edition was published in 1725 without revision, and a third edition (with minor revisions) was published together with the second edition of the *Principles* in 1734.

An Essay Towards a New Theory of Vision (1709) and The Theory of Vision . . . Vindicated and Explained (1733)

Berkeley's first major publication, his *Essay Towards a New Theory of Vision* (sometimes referred to as the *Essay on Vision*, the *Essay* or the *New Theory of Vision*) should be mentioned as it seems to be a 'halfway house' on the road to Berkeley's full denial of the existence of matter in the *Principles* and the *Dialogues*.

The *New Theory of Vision* is principally a work on the philosophy of sense perception, and specifically on the philosophy of vision. In it, Berkeley attacks the traditional account of the way we come to see objects as being a given distance from us, and as having a given size and orientation, and in its place he offers us a new explanation. *En route*, he argues that the things our faculty of sight tells us about in the first instance are nothing other than ideas, and as such can only exist in the mind. He also argues that it is in fact our sense of *touch*, and not our sense of *vision*, which ultimately informs us that objects exist at a distance from us, and that the things we see in the first instance are nothing like the things we touch.

Should you read the *New Theory of Vision*, however, you need to take care. Taken at face value it falls short of a full statement of Berkeley's denial of the existence of matter. While he argues here that the things our sense of *vision* tells us about in the first instance are nothing other than ideas that only exist in the mind, Berkeley doesn't deny, and in fact he implies, that the things our sense of *touch* tells us about are material objects that exist beyond the mind, out there in the external world. In the *Principles*, published in the following year, Berkeley *does* deny that the things our sense of touch tells us about are material objects; indeed, he denies that there can be any such thing as matter in existence. So, at first it might look as though he changed his mind in between writing the *New Theory of Vision* and the *Principles*. However, Berkeley himself says that this is not so. At §44 of the *Principles*, he tells us that he had deliberately refrained from playing all his cards in the *New Theory of Vision*, and that while he believed all along that there could be no such thing as matter in existence, he'd had his reasons for not saying so at that particular point. Some Berkeley scholars don't quite take him at his word here. Nonetheless, the standard view is that he was telling the truth, and consequently that while some of his philosophy in the *New Theory of Vision* on the surface seems to contradict what he says in the *Principles* and the

Dialogues, in fact we are ultimately presented with a consistent and unified account across all three books.

What can't be disputed is that in 1733 Berkeley published a short piece, the *Theory of Vision . . . Vindicated and Explained*, in which he endeavours to reconcile his full denial of the existence of matter in the *Principles* and the *Dialogues* with the seemingly 'halfway house' philosophy of the *New Theory of Vision*. He had republished the *New Theory of Vision* in 1732, by including it as an appendix to his theological work *Alciphron*. Consequently, a rather harshly worded review of the *New Theory of Vision* had appeared in a newspaper later that year, to which the *Theory of Vision . . . Vindicated and Explained* was Berkeley's response. In it, Berkeley makes it quite clear that the interim claim in the *New Theory of Vision* that the things we see in the first instance are nothing other than ideas is consistent with, and indeed should be supplemented with, his full blown denial of the existence of matter in the *Principles*. In its turn, the *Theory of Vision . . . Vindicated and Explained* is also consistent with Berkeley's philosophy in the *Principles* and the *Dialogues*, and there are occasionally passages in the former which help shed light on some of the claims in his two main philosophical works.

The Philosophical Commentaries (written in 1707–1708, though unpublished in Berkeley's lifetime)

When he was preparing the *New Theory of Vision* and the *Principles*, Berkeley kept a pair of notebooks, in which he recorded the philosophical thoughts he was having, memos concerning the style, content and layout of the two books, and various other bits and bats. There are approximately 900 entries in the notebooks, many of which are at most just two or three sentences in length, and most of them have a symbol in the margin indicating either the philosophical topic that the entry concerns, or what Berkeley intended to do with the entry in question (for example whether or not he should discard it).

The notebooks were only rediscovered in the nineteenth century, and were published for the first time in 1871 as part of A. C. Fraser's edition of Berkeley's complete works. Fraser entitled them Berkeley's 'Commonplace Book', but they were renamed the *Philosophical Commentaries* by A. A. Luce in 1944, and the name has stuck ever since.

Students coming to study Berkeley for the first time don't really have any business reading the *Philosophical Commentaries*, at least not until they have really got on top of Berkeley's philosophy, and have a desire to research his work in more detail. That said, a great deal of care needs to be taken if and when you do decide to read them. It is certainly true that they offer a fascinating and illuminating insight into Berkeley's mind at the point in his life when he was really thinking through and developing the philosophical ideas for which he became famous. Through them we come to learn a lot about his influences, his bugbears and the difficulties, both philosophical and stylistic that he had to wrestle with when preparing his first two major books. We see him changing his mind, revising his views and temporarily adopting positions that he would ultimately go on to reject. And for these reasons, using entries from the *Philosophical Commentaries* as evidence that Berkeley believed this, that or the other is a risky business – it's not always the case that what he wrote in them is what he ultimately believed. Nonetheless, used with due care, the *Philosophical Commentaries* can be a very useful resource for more advanced students of Berkeley.

Other main published works

Berkeley's first main publication after the *Dialogues* was his essay *De Motu* ('of motion'), which he published in 1721. He had originally entered it in a prize essay competition run by the French Academy in 1720 (which he didn't win), on his way back from his Grand Tour of Continental Europe. It's written in Latin (but has since been translated into English), and in it Berkeley addresses some problems in physics concerning motion, in the light of his denial of the existence of matter.

Alciphron (1732), like the *Dialogues*, was written in dialogue form, purporting to be a conversation between four characters over seven Dialogues. There is a reasonable amount of philosophy of religion in *Alciphron*, and in it Berkeley also repeats his attack, from the *Principles* and the *Dialogues*, against the possibility of entertaining certain kinds of 'abstract idea'. As I've already mentioned, Berkeley included a new edition of his *New Theory of Vision* as an appendix to the three editions of *Alciphron* published in 1732, as the latter work at one point touches on some of his claims about vision that he made in the former. Unlike his previous writings, *Alciphron* provoked an immediate debate in 'the republic of letters' (*i.e.*, people published written responses to it).

In *The Analyst* (1734), Berkeley attacks a theory in mathematics which entails infinitesimally small rates of speed. His concern in doing so was two-fold. Belief in the possibility of the infinitesimally small went hand-in-hand with belief in matter, which was typically held to be infinitely divisible. Since Berkeley denied the existence of matter, here and often elsewhere he is keen to deny the possibility of the infinitesimally small. He was also keen to refute the view that Christian belief is untenable since it requires the acceptance of 'mysteries' (such as the doctrine of the Trinity). Hence he argues in the *Analyst* that Christianity is no more mysterious than mathematics given the latter's insistence on mind-boggling entities such as the infinitesimally small, and that people who are prepared to believe in the mathematics of the day should have no problem believing in Christianity. Much like *Alciphron* before it, *The Analyst* also provoked a published controversy.

One of his publications that best demonstrated Berkeley's concern with practical matters and the welfare of his fellow man was *The Querist*, a tract that consists entirely of rhetorical questions, and which addresses numerous issues in economics. Written soon after he was appointed Bishop of Cloyne, Berkeley originally published *The Querist* in three parts between 1735 and 1737, reissuing it in a single, abridged volume in 1750. His overriding concern in doing so was to alleviate the plight of the poor in Ireland, and many of the suggestions implied by his questions were recognized as being particularly appropriate and practicable at the time.

The final book I want to mention is *Siris* (1744), which is by some way Berkeley's strangest work. It's a hotchpotch of material, some of it philosophical or theological, some of it scientific and some of it concerning the virtues of 'tar water' as a medicinal cure-all. In terms of the philosophy contained in *Siris*, at a first glance Berkeley perhaps seems to have performed something of u-turn, apparently advocating various doctrines that he had vigorously denied in his earlier works. At a second glance, however, this is maybe not so, and a case can be (and has been) made for this change of heart being merely apparent.

iii. HOW TO STUDY THE HISTORY OF PHILOSOPHY AND HOW TO USE THIS BOOK

Getting to grips with thinkers who lived hundreds of years ago is tricky. Working out what they said, let alone thinking critically about whether or not you're persuaded by any of it, takes a good deal of patience and involves many potential pitfalls. For instance, these people often use words and terms that had a (sometimes radically) different meaning back then from the meaning we are used to today, and they are often writing and thinking against a backdrop of old-fashioned and archaic theories and assumptions that we can easily lose sight of ourselves. In this section I'm going to give you some tips on how to go about studying famous, long-dead philosophers in general, and Berkeley in particular.

Reading and re-reading the 'primary texts'

You might think, given what I've just told you, that reading Berkeley's books *before* you've come to a good understanding of the philosophical and intellectual climate in which he lived would be a bad idea. Yet reading the *Principles* and the *Dialogues* is precisely what you should do first. It's important that you familiarize yourself with what he himself says, even if some of it, or maybe even much of it, leaves you perplexed to start with. Indeed, as a general rule which I can't stress enough, when it comes to studying figures from the History of Philosophy there really is no substitute for reading what we call the 'primary literature' or the 'primary texts' (that is, the things these people actually wrote). Both the *Principles* and the *Dialogues* are relatively short books, certainly compared with some of the major works of other philosophers from the seventeenth and eighteenth centuries; you can read each of Berkeley's main books through in a day. Then, when you're thinking about his philosophy later on, perhaps in preparation for a tutorial or seminar, or in the light of what you've heard in a lecture, or while you're reading a book like mine, you should have a copy of the *Principles* and the *Dialogues* to hand. This will allow you to re-read relevant sections and so keep in mind *what Berkeley actually said*. As you progress, and your understanding of Berkeley's philosophy improves, you should occasionally re-read whole sections or perhaps even all of one and/or the other.

It is also important that you work out what *you* take Berkeley to be saying, and by this I've two things in mind here. First, while you shouldn't worry about taking notes when you first read the *Principles* and the *Dialogues*, later on when you're trying to get your head around a given claim, theory or argument, it's often a good idea to test your understanding by writing down (in your own words as much as possible) what you take Berkeley's point to be. Sometimes it's only when you try to explain a given claim, theory or argument to someone else that you really find out whether *you've* understood it. And you can practice explaining that claim, theory or argument to someone else by explaining it to yourself first. Writing down what you're trying to think clearly about is an excellent way of testing how much you've comprehended. But don't just copy out the way Berkeley says something (although you'll inevitably have to use some of his words and terms). Perhaps put your copy of his book to one side while you try to write down the point(s) in question – you can always pick it up again if you need a reminder.

The second thing I have in mind when I recommend that you should work out what *you* take Berkeley to be saying is this. Sometimes it's just not clear from the primary texts exactly what he means when he makes a given point. So, people who write about Berkeley often *disagree* about what he means when he says this, that or the other. In short, there's plenty of scope for a novice reader of Berkeley to get confused both by what Berkeley himself says, and by what others take him to be saying. If you find that you're confused by a particular passage, work out what you think is the most likely meaning, and back up your interpretation with the odd quotation from the primary texts. Let what other people say guide you here, by all means; but don't take your eye off what Berkeley himself actually wrote. And of course if in the fullness of time you come to think that the passage in question means something different you can always change your mind.

Using the 'secondary literature'

After you've read the *Principles* and the *Dialogues* once through, a good place to turn next in coming to understand Berkeley's philosophy is what we call the 'secondary literature' – that is, things written about him by other people. There are three main kinds of secondary literature: (a) Books (or chapters in books) like mine that are dedicated to Berkeley's philosophy in general, or to various aspects of his philosophy in particular; (b) Articles or papers either in academic journals, or in 'edited collections' (books that are made up of pieces written by different people on a given topic, and which are put together by the editor(s) named on the front cover); (c) Entries in encyclopaedias and academic dictionaries, available either in book form or online.

To say a little bit about each of these resources in reverse order, entries in encyclopaedias and academic dictionaries can be useful starting points. They tend to offer brief and general overviews of Berkeley's philosophy and most will be appropriately pitched at beginners. Typically they won't give you a great deal, if anything, by way of food for thought for working out what *you think* of Berkeley's arguments. One resource in particular that you need to take some care with is *Wikipedia*, and that goes for what it has to say about any philosophical topic or thinker. While *Wikipedia* can be a mine of useful information on many topics, you should bear in mind that it isn't 'peer-reviewed' in any robust sense (that is, its content doesn't have to be approved by experts before it is posted). In principle, anyone can post or edit material on *Wikipedia*, so there's no *guarantee* that the material you read is accurate or appropriate. This is particularly the case with entries on philosophy, given the degree of expertise required to master the subject. If you do choose to use *Wikipedia* to find out about a philosophical topic or thinker, I would urge you to take it solely as a starting point, and don't take what you read as gospel truth.

As a general rule, articles or papers in academic journals or edited collections are likely to be an inappropriate starting point for students coming to study Berkeley's philosophy for the first time. Much of the very best Berkeley scholarship has taken this form. Nonetheless, these resources tend to be narrowly focused on particular sections of Berkeley's thought, and tend to assume (often a great deal of) background knowledge. If you were to simply dive in and start to read articles and papers on Berkeley's philosophy without any guidance as to which pieces might be more suited to your needs, odds on you'd soon be lost, flummoxed and bored. That said, there are some really excellent articles and papers out there which, while typically more suited to more advanced students of Berkeley, you might find useful. If you do want to use this kind of resource, a good way to identify appropriate pieces is to keep your eye out for those that are mentioned again and again in the books you're reading, especially if these mentions are accompanied by comments like 'an excellent yet straightforward paper to read if you are interested in this topic'.

The most appropriate kind of secondary literature for students coming to study Berkeley for the first time is books on Berkeley; that is, books other than the edited collections of articles and papers that I've talked about above. Sometimes referred to as 'commentaries' (written by 'commentators'), there are all manner of books on Berkeley's philosophy, some more suitable for beginners than others, and some more general than others. Your best bet here is to get hold of two or three basic, general commentaries on Berkeley, and I've included my own recommendations in Appendix B at the end of this book. It won't necessarily be a good idea to read a given commentary straight through from cover to cover, and in fact not many people do. Perhaps it's the case that you are particularly interested in reading more about a certain portion of Berkeley's philosophy or a certain argument that he gives us. In which case, narrowing down your reading by consulting the book's table of contents or index might be a better idea.

The secondary literature in general is there in the first place to help you improve your own understanding of Berkeley's philosophy. That said, don't just blindly accept what a given author says Berkeley means though. Different authors say different things, and they can't all be right. Don't forget to compare the interpretations you find in the secondary literature with your own interpretation and with what Berkeley himself says in the primary texts. If you think on reflection that a given author's interpretation is mistaken and you can say why, for example by backing yourself up with quotations from the primary texts, then good for you. In the second place, the secondary literature is there to help you decide whether or not you're persuaded by what Berkeley says. What you'll often find when you read books or papers on Berkeley is authors attacking him by presenting objections to his claims, or defending him by presenting replies to these objections. Again, don't just blindly accept a given objection or reply though – have a think about whether or not the author in question has done enough to convince you that he or she has got a good point. If you think that he or she's got it wrong and you can say why, again that's great – you're joining in the debate and actually doing some philosophy yourself. Finally, the various claims that you find in the secondary literature are there for you to mobilize yourself when you come to formulate your own assessment of Berkeley's philosophy. Of course you shouldn't risk committing plagiarism by presenting someone else's claims as if they were your own. But it's perfectly appropriate for you to say, if for example you're not convinced by one of Berkeley's arguments, that the argument is vulnerable to an objection articulated in this book by Professor Bloggs.

Being nice to the dead – the role of charitable interpretation in the History of Philosophy

One of the main reasons why studying figures from the History of Philosophy is challenging (and interesting) is that they are often working and thinking in a different intellectual climate from our own. Berkeley took certain beliefs and assumptions to be obviously true that we may not have even contemplated. He signs up to various philosophical theories and views that were commonplace in his day, but which have long since fallen out of fashion and into obscurity. So, we sometimes unquestioningly accept philosophical views that only came into currency after Berkeley's death, views that (perhaps unconsciously) deeply permeate the ways we think about the world today. Given this, how can we possibly hope to come to any objective appreciation and assessment of his philosophy?

One way is by becoming acquainted with, and hopefully coming to understand, the prevailing philosophical assumptions and theories that were held when Berkeley was alive, and introducing you to this kind of background material is one of the purposes of this book. Another way is by adopting an appropriately *sympathetic* and *charitable* attitude to Berkeley's philosophy. Some people rapidly latch on to the conclusion that Berkeley's arguments are 'just stupid'. But as a general rule, I'd strongly urge this: anyone who thinks that a famous dead philosopher's arguments are 'just stupid' probably hasn't understood them properly. Don't forget that figures like Berkeley were very clever people indeed – their thinking has stood the test of time for a good reason. So, one thing I have in mind when I recommend adopting an appropriately sympathetic and charitable attitude to Berkeley's philosophy is that you should be willing to credit him with the strongest possible arguments that are consistent with what he says. For example, if it strikes you that a given argument could be interpreted in two different ways, one of which sees him saying something daft, and the other sees him saying something clever, then (everything else being equal) be generous and give him the benefit of the doubt.

And *because* Berkeley was operating in an intellectual context somewhat different from our own, we need to do something more than assess the success or otherwise of his arguments *by our own standards*, when we come to think critically about what he says. Of course, it *is* perfectly appropriate to ask whether or not we are personally persuaded by what Berkeley had to say, and it's inevitable that in doing so we bring to bear what has come to be known since his day. But we can also assess Berkeley's claims and arguments *on his own terms*. If you like, we can put on our eighteenth-century shoes by temporarily granting him the philosophical theories and assumptions that were commonly accepted back then, and ask *in that context* whether his arguments are any good.

This is especially important given the central role that Berkeley and many of his contemporaries gave to God in their philosophical systems. One extremely quick way to do away with Berkeley's own philosophical system (though not his arguments against the existence of matter, which don't depend on the existence of God) is to protest that 'I don't believe in God, so I'm going to reject what he says out of hand'. But even if you don't believe in God, you can still ask what, if anything, is wrong with Berkeley's arguments for the existence of God. And temporarily granting Berkeley the existence of God for the sake of argument and asking on *that* basis whether or not his claims and arguments are any good is one of the main ways in which you can adopt an appropriately sympathetic and charitable attitude towards his philosophy. Once you've finished assessing Berkeley's work on his own terms, *then* it's time to revoke the assumptions that you'd temporarily granted him, and to move on to engage with him on *your* terms by asking how his views compare to yours, and by trying to disprove what he says if you happen to disagree with him.

Critically assessing Berkeley's philosophy

Once you've read what Berkeley has to say, and you've worked out what exactly his philosophical claims and arguments are, you'll be in a position to work out what you think of them. Are you persuaded by him? If you aren't, then you face the challenge of saying where exactly he has gone wrong. If you are persuaded by him, then your challenge is to try to defend what he says against critics who do think he has gone wrong. Either way, you need to be nice and precise in stating what his arguments are, and what, if anything, is wrong with them. Here is a quick summary of some of the basic questions you can ask when you're trying to decide whether you're persuaded by what Berkeley says.

- Has he presented you with an ***argument*** for a given claim, or has the claim merely been *stated* or *asserted* without argument?

Technically speaking, an argument in philosophy is a set of statements, one of which is the **conclusion** (the claim that the person giving the argument is trying to persuade you to accept) and the others are **premises** (the reasons you've been given for why you should accept the conclusion in question).

- If Berkeley has given us an *argument*, are its premises **true**? If one or more of the crucial premises (*i.e.*, if one or more of the key reasons we've been given for why we should accept the argument's conclusion) turn out to be **false**, then we can hardly be expected to be persuaded by *this* particular argument to accept the conclusion in question. (Although there may be *other* arguments for the same conclusion that do persuade us.)
- If Berkeley has given us an *argument*, does he intend the premises by themselves to guarantee 100% that the conclusion is true (in which case it's a **deductive** argument), or does he intend the premises to establish only that the conclusion is *probably* true (in which case it's an **inductive** argument).
- If he's given us an *inductive* argument, we can ask this further question: On the *hypothetical assumption* that the premises are true, do they by themselves successfully establish that the conclusion is probably true? As a general rule, if the answer to this question is 'yes' AND the premises *are in fact true*, then we've been given a good inductive argument, and we are rationally obliged to accept that the conclusion is probably true.
- If he's given us a *deductive* argument, do the premises in fact support the conclusion? That is, on the *hypothetical assumption* that the premises are true, do they by themselves guarantee 100% that the conclusion would also be true? If they do, it's known as a **valid** argument. Otherwise, it's an **invalid** argument, and it shouldn't persuade anyone. One good way to test whether a given argument is valid or not is to try to think of a **counterexample** – can you think of a scenario in which the premises of the argument would be true, and yet the conclusion would be false? If you can, then you've shown that the argument in question is invalid – because your counterexample is living proof that the assumed truth of the premises *doesn't* guarantee 100% that the conclusion would also be true.

- Some *valid* arguments are rubbish arguments, however. Even if an argument's premises (on the *hypothetical assumption* that they are true) *do* by themselves guarantee 100% that the conclusion would also be true, we still need to ask again whether or not the premises are in fact true. If a valid argument has a crucial premise which turns out to be false (*i.e.*, hypothetical assumptions aside), then the argument's no good. A *valid* argument whose premises do happen to be true though is known as a **sound** argument. All invalid arguments, and all valid arguments with a crucial premise that turns out to be false, are **unsound** arguments, and shouldn't persuade anyone. As a general rule though, if Berkeley has presented us with a *sound* argument, we've been presented with an argument which has nothing wrong with it, and whose conclusion we're thereby rationally obliged to accept.

- One exception to this rule, and another way in which an argument can be flawed (even if it's a sound argument), is when we have a **circular argument** on our hands. A circular argument is one whose conclusion itself appears (perhaps implicitly) as part of the very reasoning that's used to establish that the conclusion is true (or probably true). 'It says in the Bible that God exists; therefore God exists' is a circular argument, because we can only jump from the premise (that it says in the Bible that God exists) to the conclusion (that God exists) if we already accept that God exists (and that He guarantees the truth of what is written in the Bible). A circular argument, even if it is a sound argument, is no good for convincing people who aren't already persuaded that the conclusion is true. Do any of Berkeley's arguments strike you as circular in this way?

- Is a given claim that Berkeley makes **plausible**? That is, does it fit with your *common-sense* beliefs about the world (and with the other *philosophical* commitments that you have)? If the answer to this last question is 'no', then you may be justified in rejecting the claim in question as **implausible**. This is a good question to ask if Berkeley *hasn't* given us an argument for the claim, or if he has, but the argument turns out to be a weak one. By asking whether the claim is plausible, you're essentially asking whether you might be prepared to accept it anyway, in the absence of a decent supporting argument. Indeed, *even if* Berkeley has given us a *sound* argument for a given claim, then the argument might still run into problems, for example in the case that it's an argument for a claim that no one in their right mind is going to accept. (David Hume, the famous eighteenth-century Scottish philosopher, wrote of Berkeley's arguments in this way – 'they admit of no answer and produce no conviction' – *An Enquiry Concerning Human Understanding*, Section 12, Part 2, footnote to paragraph 122.) An argument for a claim that no one in their right mind is going to accept (even if it's a sound argument) is a ***self-refuting argument***.

- Be careful though – if something Berkeley says is at odds with one of your own beliefs about the world, are you sure that it's Berkeley's claim that you should reject, rather than your own belief? Sometimes the job of philosophy is to challenge parts of our everyday, common-sense thinking, and to expose as unjustified, irrational prejudices some of our beliefs that we perhaps never really think about critically. So if there's a clash between one of Berkeley's claims and one of your own common-sense beliefs (or one of your other philosophical views), ask yourself whether or not there are *good reasons* for thinking that your belief is in fact true. Can you provide a *rational justification* for your view? For instance, can you *prove* that your view is true by providing a decent *argument* which establishes that it is? If you can't, then your own belief might turn out to be nothing more than a prejudice that you've unthinkingly accepted just because lots of other people hold the same belief. In short, don't be overly hasty in rejecting Berkeley's views as *implausible*. Are they any less plausible than your own?
- Are Berkeley's claims **consistent** with one another? Or does he contradict himself at any point? Take two or more of his claims, and *assume for the sake of argument* that they are true. If any of the claims contradict one another, then they are ***inconsistent***, and we know for sure that at least one of them is in fact false and has to go. But which one(s)? If we're being appropriately charitable to Berkeley then (everything else being

equal) we should reject the claim(s) whose loss would do the least damage to his overall system. Once we've rejected the claim(s) in question, we can then ask whether or not their loss has done *irreparable* damage to his philosophy.

How to use the rest of this book

In the next chapter I'm going to fill you in on some of the important background theories, assumptions and thinkers that provoked and inspired Berkeley to write what he did. Having done that, I'm then going to move on in the main part of the book to guide you through the main arguments, claims and theories that you'll find in the *Principles* and the *Dialogues*. Chapter 3 is devoted to what we might call Berkeley's 'positive' philosophy – his account of what there is in existence, how we arrive at knowledge of what there is, and how he takes his system to be in tune with our common-sense beliefs about the world. In Chapter 4 I'll be presenting the main arguments and other strategies by which he aims to prove that there can be no such thing as matter, and that everyday objects are in fact nothing other than collections of ideas.

I am going to impose a certain structure on his claims and arguments, one which I think fits best with the primary texts, and in doing so I'm giving you my interpretation of what he says. This is my attempt to show you a helpful way to think about Berkeley's philosophy, with the aim of improving your understanding of what you'll find when you read his books – I'm essentially saying 'try thinking about it this way'.

Along the way, I will also be presenting some of the common objections to Berkeley's philosophical moves, as well as the occasional objection of my own, and I'll be suggesting replies to some of these objections. My aim here is to get you thinking critically about what Berkeley says, and about what others have made of his views. Don't forget though that my book is part of the secondary literature, and as such you should bear in mind what I've said above concerning the secondary literature's use. Whatever I go on to say, and whatever my views happen to be, keep your mind firmly fixed on the fact that when you do the History of Philosophy by critically engaging with what Berkeley thought and wrote, the two most important opinions for you to work out are Berkeley's and your own.

Finally, rather than constantly bombarding you with quoted passages from the primary texts in an attempt to prove to you that Berkeley says what I claim he does, in the main I'll simply provide a sample of references at appropriate points that you can look up for yourself in the *Principles* and the *Dialogues*. This should give you some help when it comes to locating precisely where Berkeley himself talks about the topics we'll be covering, and it will give you the chance to decide for yourself whether you see what I claim is there to be seen. (See pp. 183–4 for details of the standard editions of the *Principles* and the *Dialogues* in use today and for a guide to the page numbers *etc.* that I'll be using in my references to them in the main part of this book.)

CHAPTER 2

BERKELEY'S INFLUENCES: KEY FIGURES AND THEORIES

Berkeley was an early Modern Philosopher – that is, he was writing and thinking in (and against the intellectual backdrop of) the early part of what is called the Modern period of Western Philosophy. Modern Philosophy, perhaps confusingly, started in the seventeenth century, and the early Modern Philosophers defined themselves as such in relation to what had gone before. And what had gone before were centuries of thought dominated by a (sometimes slavish) acceptance of the philosophy of the ancient Greek thinker Aristotle (384–322 BC). The period that preceded Modern Philosophy is also known as the Scholastic era, because this Aristotle-driven philosophy was what was taught in the 'Schools' – the early universities.

People today disagree about when the Modern period of philosophy came to an end, or indeed whether or not it has yet come to an end. Whatever the case may be, it's helpful to refer to the up-to-date philosophy that is being done today as Contemporary Philosophy, and it's common to use the term Modern Philosophy when talking especially about the seventeenth and eighteenth centuries.

The start of the Modern period was marked by a willingness to move away from what had bordered on a blind acceptance of what Aristotle had said. The new philosophers urged us to work things out for ourselves, rather than relying on what authority figures happened to say. (The emergence of Modern Philosophy went hand-in-hand with the rise of the new science led by the likes of Galileo and Newton. Indeed, many of these new scientists were also philosophers – the two disciplines were far less clearly distinguished than they are today. This was a time when philosophy was known as the 'queen of the sciences', and science was called 'natural philosophy'.) Consequently there was a fresh emphasis on doing things for oneself, both in philosophy and in science. And when philosophers started to think for themselves, rather than relying on what traditional authorities told them, in conjunction with the discoveries of the science of the day, philosophy began to evolve away, sometimes quite radically, from the antiquated views of Aristotle.

By the time Berkeley came along, Modern Philosophy was well underway, to the extent that the reputation of the founding fathers of the era had been established, and Modern thought itself had begun to evolve in its turn. There were critical reactions, both positive and negative, to the theories of the first Modern Philosophers. With Berkeley, we find a philosopher writing his major works in the early years of the eighteenth century, who was both deeply impressed by some of the things that his seventeenth-century predecessors had said, but who would also vehemently reject some of their central commitments. His main worry was that the new philosophy, far from establishing human knowledge on a fresh footing, would in fact cut us off from having any certain knowledge whatsoever, and worse, risked cutting us off from God. The result, in the form of his philosophical theories of immaterialism (the view that there is no such thing as matter) and idealism (the view that everyday objects are ideas in the mind), is one of the most challenging, revolutionary, and for many people downright strange accounts of the world ever produced. (However, even in his own time he was up against some pretty stiff competition here – just check out what the German philosopher Gottfried Wilhelm Leibniz (1646–1716) or the Dutch philosopher Baruch Spinoza (1632–77) had to say if wacky philosophical theories are your thing.)

Berkeley is also an 'Empiricist' philosopher. Indeed, he's described as one of the three big 'British Empiricists' of the day, along with John Locke and David Hume. (The fact that Berkeley was Irish and that Ireland wasn't formally part of Britain when he was alive seems to have been overlooked). Empiricism is a broad tradition in philosophy, and is contrasted with 'Rationalism', with many of the philosophers of the early Modern period being cast as members of one tradition or the other. There's some disagreement about quite how each tradition should be defined, and moreover about whether it's accurate to say that there was any clean-cut dichotomy between any two such traditions at all. For our purposes though it's enough to say that the Empiricist tradition is character- ized by the claim that all of our knowledge derives from what our five senses tell us. The Rationalist tradition in turn is characterized by the claim that while it may be the case that without our five senses we couldn't come to know anything at all, the story doesn't end there – Rationalists typically claim that our faculty of reason can give us knowledge beyond what we find out via sense experience.

In the first half of the rest of this chapter, I am going to introduce three philosophers – René Descartes, Nicolas Malebranche and John Locke – whose work, either directly or indirectly, had a pro- found influence on Berkeley. It's clear, from what we know of Berkeley's university education, and from the mentions he makes of these thinkers in his writings, notebooks and letters, that he had read and was very familiar with their major philosophical works. Nonetheless, the precise extent to which they *directly* inspired him to write what he did (in the sense that he either accepted or rejected their views as a direct result of having read them) is hard to deter- mine. Where he wasn't directly influenced though, Berkeley would certainly have been indirectly influenced by these three philosophers insofar as they contributed significantly to the philosophical agenda of the time, and to the canon of doctrines that were commonly accepted, to a greater or lesser extent, in Berkeley's day.

It's fair to say that Locke and Malebranche directly influenced his thinking the most. A crude and misleading characterization is that Berkeley's philosophy was solely a reaction against what Locke had written before him. But while it is the case that Berkeley often has Locke in his sights (or at least the kinds of theory of which Locke's philosophy is representative), there are also important parts of Locke's thinking with which Berkeley would whole-heartedly agree. That said, the extent to which Malebranche's writings inspired Berkeley to start thinking in immaterialist and idealist ways (even though Malebranche himself wasn't an immaterialist or an idealist) is often underestimated.

There were, of course, many other thinkers whose work influenced Berkeley – I include Descartes, Malebranche and Locke as the three most significant. Having given you a general overview of some of their particular positions, I will then move on in the second half of this chapter to describe some further philosophical issues, and some doctrines that by Berkeley's time were widely accepted, which form the background to many of the things that he himself would have to say. In this way, having come to some sort of appreciation of the context in which Berkeley was writing, we'll be better placed in subsequent chapters to understand his own theories and arguments.

i. RENÉ DESCARTES (1596–1650)

The French philosopher René Descartes is often called 'the Father of Modern Philosophy', such was his pioneering role in moving away from the reliance on authority figures, and indeed the philosophical methods and doctrines, that had dominated during the Scholastic period. He is most famous for the dictum *cogito, ergo sum*, or 'I think, therefore I am', by which he intended to establish that you know beyond doubt that you exist whenever you think. (Try doubting that you exist, he says, and you'll only succeed in proving your own existence afresh – after all, you must be around to do the doubting). Descartes didn't intend the *Cogito* (as this move has become known) merely to be some trivial observation. Instead, he took it to be the founding stone on which he could build his entire philosophical system, and in the process *prove* that there are very many things that we can know for certain despite the claims of those who say otherwise, and that doing science/philosophy is the way we can go about coming to know them. Descartes' major writings were his *Discourse on Method* (1637), his *Meditations on First Philosophy* (1641) – often referred to simply as the *Meditations* – and his *Principles of Philosophy* (1644).

As you may well have gathered from what I've already said, Descartes was particularly worried about the threat of 'Scepticism' – the claim that many of our cherished beliefs are open to doubt, and that we *can't* know for sure some, or perhaps many, or maybe even all of the things that we think we do know. Scepticism had become somewhat fashionable among intellectuals in Descartes' day – after all, this was a time when there was great upheaval intellectually and in social and political life in general. The traditional authority of the Catholic Church had been thrown into doubt following the Reformation, a new science was on the rise, and in many other spheres of life what had previously been believed and done was being challenged and overturned. Descartes was convinced that if the new science was to be placed on a secure footing, Scepticism had to be defeated. Berkeley shared this desire to see Scepticism defeated, although he thought that it was the new philosophy itself, championed by people like Descartes, which risked stranding us in the very Scepticism that it aimed to combat.

One specific kind of Scepticism is 'external world Scepticism'. According to the Sceptic here, we can't know for sure that what we take to be the real world around us – the world of tables and chairs and other people – actually exists. Isn't it a possibility, however remote, that what we take to be reality is in fact all just a dream, or some other kind of grand illusion? And so long as it's a possibility that 'it's all a dream', we can't be 100% certain that the real world exists – there's always going to be room for some doubt. Or so the Sceptic says. Descartes was the first Modern thinker to put the question of whether we can know for certain that the real world exists on the philosophical agenda, and it's a question that Berkeley was very much interested in. Like Descartes, he thought that we can know for certain that the real world exists, though it might strike you as strange that a philosopher who denies the existence of matter, and who claims that tables and chairs are just collections of ideas in the mind, should be committed to the view that the real world exists. Nonetheless, Berkeley was, and what's more he thought that it was the very belief in the existence of matter that made 'external world Scepticism' possible in the first place (see below, pp. 96–7).

Descartes is also one of those typically cast as a Rationalist philosopher (see above, p. 28). He thought that each of us was born with the capability to generate 'innate ideas' in our minds. Given the right kinds of experiences and education in life, he claimed, we can become aware of certain ideas (such as the idea of God) which we can then think about and manipulate in ways that will allow us to know many things which go beyond anything our sense experience tells us. What's more, Descartes denied that the five senses, by themselves, can tell us *anything at all* about the world. In the second of his *Meditations,* he famously uses the example of a piece of wax which melts when it's near the fire. Everything our senses tell us about the wax in its solid state, for example that it is hard to the touch and that it has a certain shape and colour, changes once it melts. Yet we still know that it is the same wax. Since everything our senses tell us about changes, while we still know it's the same wax, it can't be the case that we know this via our senses. According to Descartes, it's only when the mind, by means of the innate ideas of the faculty of reason, *interprets* what the senses give us that we can come to know anything for certain on that basis. This relegation of the role our sense experience plays in providing us with knowledge about the world was something that Berkeley the Empiricist would be very keen to reverse. He thought that we *can* trust our senses to tell us the way things really are, and he took this notion that we can entertain thoughts that are entirely independent of the testimony of the senses to be the root of all manner of mistakes in philosophy.

The fact that Descartes placed our own thoughts (such as the *Cogito*) and our innate ideas at the starting point in our quest for knowledge saw him embarking on a radical new departure in philosophy – what since has been dubbed the 'Way of Ideas'. For him, and indeed for very many Modern philosophers through to Berkeley and beyond, it is our own ideas and mental experiences that we are aware of first and foremost in our attempts to come to know about the world around us, including when we perceive things using our senses (see the section on 'Indirect Realism' below, pp. 44–6). But whereas Descartes thought that these ideas and mental experiences could allow us to infer the further existence of a material world, Berkeley would argue that the real world simply *was* (certain of) our ideas and experiences.

Descartes, like Berkeley, also places God at the heart of much of his philosophy. Or at least he seems to. He certainly attempts to prove the existence of God by philosophical argument. And his standard published story is that it is only via knowledge of God that we can come to know anything else for certain. However, some of Descartes' writings also give the impression that he thought that God created the material universe at the start of time, instituted the three laws of motion that Descartes thought governed the behaviour of all material objects, and then stepped back and let matter take care of itself from thereon in (bar the odd miracle). This thought (whether in Descartes' words or not), that the behaviour of matter could be fully explained by scientific laws without further reference to the presence of God, would deeply trouble Berkeley, and constituted one of the reasons why he wanted to do away with matter. Berkeley's worry was that the new philosophy, in attempting to reconcile the existence of God with the scientific explanation of the world around us, would leave the door open for the omission of God from the picture altogether (see below, p. 170).

Finally, one way in which Descartes, or at least his legacy, influenced Berkeley in a positive sense was in the insistence that the mind is an immaterial thing whose essential nature consists in thinking. For Descartes, the mind is entirely distinct from matter. Unlike matter, minds aren't extended (or 'spread out') in space, and hence aren't divisible into parts; and minds alone are capable of thought. And since Descartes believed that to die is to break down into parts, he believed that minds are immortal – once a mind has been created, only a fiat of God's will can cause it to cease to exist. This commitment to the immaterial nature of the immortal mind, whose existence essentially consisted in thinking, would be one that Berkeley shared.

ii. NICOLAS MALEBRANCHE (1638–1715)

Father Nicolas Malebranche (whom Berkeley didn't kill) was another French philosopher, and also a priest. He was a 'Cartesian' philosopher – that is, a follower of Descartes. Indeed, he was arguably the pre-eminent Cartesian philosopher, and it's for this that he's primarily known. However, he's also an important philosopher in his own right, and he certainly had a big (though often under-acknowledged) impact on Berkeley's thinking. While Malebranche maintained and helped to clarify many of the central tenets of Descartes' philosophy, it's in those places where he diverged from Descartes that his influence on Berkeley can be most easily seen. His principle work was his *Search after Truth*, which was first published in two parts in 1674 and 1675 respectively.

Some of the early readers of Berkeley's *Principles* and *Dialogues* concluded that he was in fact a disciple of Malebranche's philosophy, which Berkeley himself strongly denied. And indeed many of Malebranche's core beliefs Berkeley did not and could not accept. Nonetheless, there are also key areas in which the two philosophers *were* in agreement, and where in all probability what Malebranche wrote directly inspired Berkeley's thinking.

For example, unlike the view often attributed to Descartes, where God takes a back seat once He's created matter and instantiated the three laws of motion which govern the behaviour of material objects, Malebranche puts God at the very heart of his philosophy, insisting that He is constantly and intimately at work in the world and in our lives. This is something that Berkeley too would urge, and in fact Malebranche regularly used a Biblical quotation in this respect that would in turn be a favourite of Berkeley's: it is God 'in whom we live and move and have our being' (Acts 17:28). It may well have been Malebranche who set Berkeley on the road to thinking that it is God's close involvement in our lives that's the key to coming to a proper philosophical understanding of the fundamental nature of the world and of our place in it.

One way in which God is at the very heart of Malebranche's philosophical system can be seen in the theory for which Malebranche is most famous his 'Occasionalism'. We think, and most people in the seventeenth-century thought, that everyday objects causally interact with one another. A billiard ball, for instance, causes a second billiard ball to move when they collide. The first ball's movement is the 'cause' that directly brings about the 'effect' of the second ball's movement. And we think, and again most people in the seventeenth century thought, that our *minds* also causally interact with material objects out there in the world. I make up my mind to lift up my arm, and lo and behold my arm lifts up. Or the mind-altering drug that I have just taken is the direct cause of the fact that

I can now see rats crawling on the ceiling. Descartes is often thought to face a problem here. Recall that according to him, the mind and matter are completely distinct from one another. For one thing, matter is extended in space, whereas the immaterial mind is not. In which case, how can a material object and the mind possibly causally interact with one another? We typically think of causal interaction in terms of objects banging into one another in physical space, like in the case of the billiard balls. But the mind, being immaterial, doesn't exist in physical space, so how can it bang into anything? How can the *force* that we typically think is required for causal interaction be transferred from a material object to my mind, or *vice versa*? Today, this conundrum is sometimes known as 'the problem of psychophysical causation'.

Malebranche gave a radical answer to these kinds of question. He denied that there is any direct causal interaction going on between different material objects, or between material objects and the mind. Instead, he maintained that God is the only genuine causal agent in existence. On his account, God sees the way the first billiard ball is behaving, and on that basis *He* brings it about that the second billiard ball starts to behave in the way it does. In Malebranche's terms, the behaviour of the first ball is the 'occasion' which prompts God to bring about the behaviour of the second. To us it still *looks* as though a genuine collision has taken place, and we can still describe what we see in terms of the laws of physics. What has *really* happened though is something else. The true explanation of what has happened sees the laws of physics only as descriptions of *God's* causal activity. What we call the 'causal interaction' between the two balls is ultimately down to God's direct intervention. Similarly, when I decide to lift my arm up and consequently it raises into the air, this isn't because my decision – an act of my mind – directly causes my arm to lift up. Instead, God sees that I've made the decision in question, and that decision is the 'occasion' which prompts God to bring it about that my arm goes up. I may say that *I* lifted my arm up, but although that is the 'natural', 'secondary' or 'occasional' cause of what happened, really the genuine cause was God.

Berkeley too would go on to argue that God is the only genuine cause of the behaviour of everyday objects like tables and chairs, and of the sensory experiences we have of them. He differs from Malebranche here in two important respects though. Malebranche holds that God is the direct cause of the behaviour of material objects, whereas Berkeley of course denies the existence of material objects. And Berkeley allows that there are *some* things that my mind can genuinely cause. For example, he thinks that I have the power to directly bring about ideas in my imagination, such as the mental image of a horse with wings. Here, it is my decision to create this image that directly causes it to pop into my mind's eye. On Malebranche's account though, even here it is God that is doing the causing – having seen that I've made my decision, God causes the image in question to appear before my mind. These differences aside though, Berkeley's belief that it is God, rather than the chair itself, that causes me to see a chair when I look across my room, and that it is God, rather than the first billiard ball, that causes the second billiard ball to start to move, is remarkably similar to, and may well have been directly inspired by, Malebranche's Occasionalism.

Another related way in which God is crucial to Malebranche's philosophy is his claim that we 'see all things in God' (or at least that we see all material things in God). Take the example of the chair I see when I look across my room again. Today we typically think that I see the chair because rays of light reflected by the chair hit my retinas, which causes electrical information to be sent down my optic nerves, which in turn causes my brain to register the presence of the chair. According to Malebranche though, what happens once the nerve-impulses reach my brain is that I become aware of the chair in its true form, as it really is, because God shares His idea of the chair with the intellectual part of my mind (as opposed to the part of my mind that deals with sensory experiences). Or at least this is what happens so long as I am being receptive to God's idea, by thinking carefully about what my senses tell me. It is this idea of God's, an idea which is of or which represents the real chair out there in the material world, which allows me to know what this particular material object is really like. As we will see, Berkeley would likewise find a central place in his philosophy for the ideas that God has of the objects in existence out there in the world, and for the claim that it is God who brings it about that we are aware of these things (although on Berkeley's account we are aware of our *own* ideas, not *God's*, when we perceive things as they really are). But in fact, Berkeley goes further than Malebranche. It's not just the case for him that God's ideas are *of*, or *represent* to us, objects like tables and chairs existing out there in the world. Rather, God's ideas, and the ideas He causes in our minds, *are* the tables and chairs – there are of course no material objects in existence for God's ideas to represent or tell us about. Quite possibly inspired by Malebranche's theory, Berkeley took things to a whole new level and dispensed with material objects altogether.

Given that Malebranche thought that we see all (material) things in God in this way, it's perhaps surprising to find out that he argued that it is impossible for us to prove by philosophical argument that material objects like tables and chairs actually exist. Unlike Descartes, who thought we could prove the existence of the external world and the objects it contains by rational argument, Malebranche thought that the only way we could come to know for certain that there are such things was by having faith in the Bible and what it says concerning their existence. Just like Descartes before him, Malebranche claims that the senses were given to us to allow us to navigate our environment and to keep us from harm; they weren't given to us to reveal to us the way material objects really are. For Descartes, it wasn't until our *intellects* interpreted what our senses tell us that we could come to know what tables and chairs were really like. To do the same job, Malebranche (as we have seen) appealed to God sharing with us His own intellectual idea of those objects. Now, the fact that Malebranche denied that philosophical argument can establish for certain that there are material objects in existence may well have helped Berkeley out here – after all, Berkeley agreed. And in fact some of the arguments Malebranche uses to this end are similar to the arguments Berkeley goes on to use in arguing for the same conclusion. Apart from the fact that Berkeley thought that we could trust our senses to tell us what objects were really like, the difference between the two philosophers here is that Berkeley also denies that faith in what the Bible has to say proves that there are material objects in existence. He tells us that nothing whatsoever in the Bible necessitates a belief in *material* objects. Tables and chairs (and snakes and fig leaves), yes; but *material* tables and chairs, no.

One other potential area of influence that should be singled out at this point concerns the possibility of contemplating 'abstract' ideas. As we will see, Berkeley denies that we can have an 'abstract general idea' of, for example, matter. That is, we can't have any idea of matter in general that doesn't make reference to, say, the size, shape and colour of some particular object or other. In saying this, Berkeley was reacting to and was completely opposed to what he took John Locke to say on this subject (see below, pp. 39–40). In Malebranche though, Berkeley would have encountered someone who, while allowing the possibility of abstract ideas, singles them out as a source of much of our mistaken thinking about the world, and who strongly warns us against their use. Despite the fact that Malebranche's own system traded on abstract entities such as 'being in general' (he took God's idea of the material world to be an idea of 'being in general'), here again he may well have set Berkeley off on his crusade against abstract ideas.

All in all, with Malebranche, Berkeley found someone with whom he was able to agree on some important points, though not others, and someone who at the very least led him to start thinking in some of the main philosophical directions he would ultimately take.

iii. JOHN LOCKE (1632–1704)

John Locke was an English philosopher, and a qualified doctor, who also wrote important works on religion, politics and economics. His major philosophical work is the gargantuan *An Essay Concerning Human Understanding* (often simply called Locke's *Essay*), which was first published in 1689 and soon made its way onto the degree syllabus which Berkeley would study at Trinity College, Dublin. A traditional yet misleading view, which I've already hinted at, is that Berkeley wrote his philosophy principally as a direct response to what Locke had said in his *Essay*, yet we've just seen how Malebranche is also a major influence on Berkeley's thinking, and in fact Berkeley rarely singles Locke out for criticism by name. Nevertheless, Locke was a huge influence on Berkeley. For one thing,

Berkeley greatly respects Locke as a philosopher, speaks of him in terms of fond admiration and in fact agrees with some of the things Locke had said in opposition to the philosophy that had gone before (including some of the views of Descartes and Malebranche). For another, even if Berkeley doesn't always have Locke himself in his sights, many of Locke's views are certainly *characteristic* of the kinds of philosophical claim that Berkeley wanted to attack.

Just like Descartes and Malebranche before him, Locke was keen to get his readers away from blindly accepting what traditional authority figures told us to think, and he insisted that we should only believe those things for which we had evidence, and which stood up to the test of reason. He conceived of himself as an 'under-labourer', as he puts it, working in the service of the science of the day by clearing away some of the philosophical rubbish that threatened to obscure and confound what scientists were trying to do. By Locke's time, 'Corpuscularianism' held sway in science. This was the view that all material objects are made up of tiny particles, or 'corpuscles', and that it was the nature and action of these corpuscles that not only ultimately explained the behaviour of larger, everyday material objects, but also caused us to experience these objects in the ways that we do. Unlike Descartes though, Locke denied that we could ever discover the *ultimate* nature of reality by doing science. For him, science was simply an extremely useful *practical* tool that helped mankind improve its lot in life. In fact he denied that we can ever discover by any means the real intrinsic nature of material objects, as they are in and of themselves, independent of the ways we encounter them to be.

Locke, like Berkeley, is traditionally cast as an Empiricist philosopher, and the two of them pretty much shared the same starting point in their thinking. Locke denied, and Berkeley agreed with him, that we had any 'innate ideas' (contrary to what Descartes had said) – ideas which the mind is at least potentially aware of from birth and whose content goes beyond what our five senses tell us. Instead, Locke conceives of the mind being a *tabula rasa* – a blank slate – at birth, waiting to receive information. And both Locke and Berkeley agreed that all of the ideas that we have, and indeed all of the knowledge that we arrive at on the basis of those ideas, derives from our experiences of the world and of ourselves. Despite their common starting point however, Locke and Berkeley would reach radically opposing conclusions, most markedly with the former asserting and the latter denying the existence of material objects.

'Ideas' are central to Locke's philosophical system, as they would be for Berkeley's, and Locke championed the 'Way of Ideas' that Descartes had pioneered. Locke, like Descartes before him, held that what we are aware of in the first instance in the process of becoming acquainted with the world around us are ideas, or episodes in the mind. It is through these ideas that we then go on to become aware of the world out there, beyond our minds. He proceeds to provide us with an 'atomistic' account of ideas, whereby we combine the 'simple ideas' that are the most basic elements (or atoms) of our perceptual experiences into more and more 'complex ideas'. For example, having received the simple ideas of a certain colour, a certain shape and a certain size from our sense experiences, we arrive at the complex idea of a horse. And once we've got hold of the complex idea of a horse and the complex idea of a horn, we can combine these into the complex idea of a unicorn. Unlike complex ideas, simple ideas can't be broken down or analysed into any more basic, constituent parts. They can't be put together or derived from other ideas that we have or other things that we know about. Instead, we can only come to possess the simple ideas that we do by having experiences of the relevant kind. On this account, I can bring someone who's never seen a zebra, for instance, to have the (rough) idea of one, by providing him or her with the component ideas of a horse and of black and white stripes. But I can't bring someone who's never seen the colour red to have the idea of the colour red in this way – there are no component ideas from which the idea of the colour red can be constructed.

Many of the theories that Locke would go on to build on the foundation of the 'Way of Ideas' are centrally important to an understanding of what Berkeley is up to in his philosophy, and we will come across some of these theories in the second half of this chapter. For now though, I want to briefly say something about a part of Locke's philosophy that Berkeley did single out for special attention and criticism – Locke's account of 'abstract general ideas'.

Locke's thinking here starts out from a commitment he has concerning language, and specifically the way words work. He claims that all meaningful words get their meaning by standing for some idea or other. To use Locke's own example, when a child learns the word 'mamma', that word has meaning for the child because it stands for the particular idea it has of its mother. However, language and indeed thought would be impossibly cumbersome if we had to come up with a different idea to represent to us each of the particular, individual things that there are in existence, and if we had to use a different word to stand for each of those particular ideas. Instead, we use general words (such as 'elephant' or 'banana') to refer wholesale to entire *classes* of the things that there are in existence. And these general words get their meaning, not by standing for this or that *particular* idea of an individual member of the class in question (*e.g.*, this particular elephant or that particular banana), but by standing for a special kind of idea – a *general* idea whose content records only those features that all individual members of the class in question have in common. So the general idea of an elephant, for instance, won't record whether or not it's an Indian elephant, or an African elephant, or an elephant with tusks, or an elephant without tusks, that we have in mind. It will only record those features that are common to all elephants. The contents of the idea – what the idea is an idea *of* or *about* – is 'abstracted' from the contents of all of the individual ideas of particular elephants that people have.

As we'll see in Chapter 4, Berkeley denied that we could have (or 'frame', to use one of his terms) any abstract general ideas of the kind that Locke describes. (In fact, Berkeley also denies that all meaningful words get their meaning by standing for an idea – see, *e.g.*, Introduction to the *Principles* §§19–20). And what's more, he thinks that this doctrine of 'abstract ideas', which he finds in Locke but which he recognizes has been around for centuries, is responsible for much of the mistaken thinking that has plagued philosophy over the years.

Having now seen some of the basic philosophical theories that characterize the work of the three philosophers whose thinking had the most profound influence on Berkeley, I want to move on next to say something about some other features of the philosophical landscape that had emerged in the seventeenth century which form part of the general backdrop to his thinking.

iv. SUBSTANCES, OBJECTS AND PROPERTIES

One question that philosophers in the seventeenth and eighteenth centuries were interested in was that of the nature of the most basic and fundamental things in existence (or 'substances', to use their term), and their relation to everyday objects like tables and chairs. As I've already hinted, Descartes maintained that ultimately there were two distinct kinds of 'substance' or two basic kinds of 'stuff' in existence, matter and minds, and it's worth expanding on his account here, before contrasting it with Locke's view, to give you a flavour of the main, rival uses of the term 'substance' that were in currency in Berkeley's time.

When it came to the material universe, Descartes said that there was ultimately just one thing in existence – a single, vast, swirling continuum of matter. This might sound odd to us – surely Descartes didn't deny that there were very many material things in existence; tables, chairs, giraffes, human bodies, blades of grass, grains of sand and so on? Well, he didn't deny that all these things existed. What he did deny was that individual tables and chairs are in any sense part of the most *basic* furniture of the universe. For Descartes, the matter which makes up tables and chairs is far more basic than this particular chair, or that particular table. And by matter here, he didn't mean the wood from which tables and chairs are made either. What he meant was the most basic stuff which makes up *all* material objects – including wooden ones, plastic ones and ones made from candyfloss or spiders' webs. Descartes used the term 'material substance' for this most basic, material 'stuff', and he said that the essential defining feature of matter was that it was extended (*i.e.*, spread out – in this case in three dimensions).

On this account tables and chairs, while not part of the most *basic* furniture of the universe, do exist. However, they don't exist in *addition* to the matter that makes them up. They are *real*, but they aren't *ultimate*. Rather, Descartes conceived of them as being ways in which the single, job-lot of material substance manifests itself in particular locations. Tables and chairs are something that matter does, different ways it expresses itself, or to use Descartes' terms, they are 'modes' or 'modifications' of matter. *We* consider a table and a chair to be two different things, whereas Descartes took them both to be manifestations of one and the same thing – extended matter.

We are also used to talking of the various features or properties that this table or that chair happens to have. For example, we might have a chair which is large and white and travelling across the room at a high speed. Or we might have a table which is oblong and flat and smells of varnish. Descartes sometimes talks of these features or properties being 'modes' or 'modifications' of the table or the chair – again, ways in which the table exists, or in which the chair manifests itself. Really though, when he restricts his focus to the fundamental nature of the material universe, he talks about these properties or features as being modifications not of tables and chairs, but of extended material substance itself. What's more, Descartes thought that there were only a restricted number of properties that matter *genuinely* had. He conceded the matter in this or that location has a given shape, size and state of motion or rest. As we'll soon see though, he thought that properties such as colour and smell were merely reactions in us, rather than *genuine* features of matter as it is in itself, out there beyond us.

And Descartes gives a similar kind of story when it comes to my mind, and its relation to what it is that all minds have in common on the one hand, and the ideas in my mind on the other. While he thinks that individual tables and chairs are in fact all manifestations of the single, extended material substance, Descartes *doesn't* think that there's just one immaterial substance, of which all individual minds are local manifestations. Along with matter, my mind is one of the very basic things that exist. Matter and my mind are both counted among the fundamental furniture of God's creation. And so is your mind, and each of your friends' minds. There's a single material continuum in existence, but multiple individual minds. The defining characteristic of minds, akin to extension in the case of matter, is thought – all minds and only minds think. The individual thoughts or ideas that I have, rather than being extra things that exist in addition to my mind, are again just ways in which my mind – my thinking thing – manifests itself. Ideas are something that minds *do*, or a way in which they exist. As tables and chairs are *modifications* of the single extended substance that is matter, so ideas are modifications of a mind.

Descartes' account of the relationship between substances, objects and properties differed from the traditional Aristotelian account that was taught in the universities in the seventeenth century, according to which the features or properties of objects, such as their colour, size and shape, 'inhered' in the substance that literally 'stands under' ('sub' – 'stance') or underlies them – analogous to the ways that pins stick in a pin cushion. On this view, the properties (the pins) are a distinct kind of entity from, and something extra that exists in addition to, the substance (the pin-cushion). On Descartes' view, the properties are ways in which a substance happens to manifest itself – the properties aren't an extra kind of thing that's in existence over and above the substance that (in the case of matter) is shaped in this way, and is moving in that way.

Locke's view differs from Descartes' in other ways. For one thing, Locke is happy for there to be many material substances, as opposed to Descartes' single material continuum. For Locke, this horse is one substance, and that horse is another. Water is a substance, and so is gold. My house is yet another, and your table is another still. These for him are the basic things and kinds of things that there are, things that exist independently from one another. It's a good question whether Locke thought that there is any more fundamental kind of material substance in existence. On occasion he tells us that we come to think that there is the substance that is this horse, or the substance that is water, simply by adding together the 'ideas' that we get from our senses of the horse's or water's various properties. There's no mention here of any 'thing' or 'substance' that exists prior to or distinct from the properties we experience. And as we'll see in Chapter 3, this account of everyday objects as collections or combinations of the properties we experience is one that would be agreeable to Berkeley.

More often however Locke seems to at least come close to

admitting that there has to be something more than just this collection of properties – there has to be some*thing*, over and above the aggregate of the properties, of which they *are* the properties. Indeed Locke tells us that our idea of any given substance includes, in addition to our ideas of its properties, some vague and altogether unclear idea of an underlying something whose properties these are. Whether or not this would be a substance in the Aristotelian sense or in the Cartesian sense he doesn't say. Suffice to note, he recognizes that there are problems with this notion of an underlying something, and Berkeley would go on to seize on the vague and altogether unclear nature of this supposed idea in arguing that there can in fact be no such thing (see below, p. 170).

To summarize then, 'substances' in the seventeenth century were taken to be the most basic things that exist, whether these were everyday material objects (or kinds of material thing), the matter underlying or manifesting itself as these, or minds. Properties were features of these things, such as the size and shape of a table or of a portion of matter, or the acts of thinking or ideas that are characteristic of a mind. And on the Cartesian account at least, properties were 'modifications' of these things – ways in which these things existed or manifested themselves.

v. INDIRECT REALISM – A POPULAR THEORY OF PERCEPTION

In light of the 'Way of Ideas' that Descartes pioneered and Locke championed, whereby it is *ideas*, or goings-on in our minds, that we are aware of in the first instance when we have the experiences that we do, Berkeley's predecessors in the seventeenth century typically held a particular theory of sense perception that's become known since as 'Indirect Realism'. Descartes, Malebranche and Locke are all commonly taken to have signed up to some version or other of this theory. According to Indirect Realism, what we are *ultimately* aware of in sense perception are *real* objects out there in the external world such as tables and chairs (hence the 'realism' part of the theory's name). However, what we are aware of in the first instance (or 'directly' or 'immediately', as is sometimes said) are mental episodes in our heads (typically called 'ideas'). It is via the ideas that we are directly aware of that we ultimately become aware of the real objects in the external world. That is, we become aware of objects like tables and chairs only *indirectly* (hence the 'indirect' part of the theory's name).

Indirect Realism is traditionally contrasted with 'Direct Realism' (sometimes called 'Naïve Realism'), according to which we are *directly* aware of real objects like tables and chairs – there are no intermediate ideas in addition to the person doing the perceiving and the tables and chairs, by means of which the former perceives the latter.

There are two main versions of Indirect Realism, which we encounter in the writings of Descartes and Locke respectively. On the one hand there is 'Inferential Realism', which is what Descartes goes for. Recall that he thinks that the senses, by themselves, tell us nothing whatsoever about the way material objects really are. It's only when our mind's faculty of reason interprets what the senses give us that we can *work out* (or *infer*) what these objects are really like. So with his famous example of the piece of wax, we don't directly *see* that the wax is essentially a portion of extended matter with a certain shape and size; what the senses give us in the first instance are 'ideas' of the wax and its properties. It's on the basis of those ideas, by thinking carefully about them, that we infer what the wax is really like.

Locke meanwhile is commonly taken to be your bog-standard 'Representative Realist'. According to Representative Realism, the ideas that we are directly aware of when we open our eyes or feel the world with our hands, *represent* to us the way the objects we are in perceptual contact with really are (or at least they do with respect to *some* of the objects' properties – namely, their 'Primary Qualities'. See the section on 'the distinction between Primary and Secondary Qualities' below, pp. 46–50). Precisely *how* the ideas represent the material objects out there is a matter of debate. The standard view, which Locke certainly seems to endorse in various places, is that the representing ideas are either like, or in fact are, little images or pictures of the objects in question, and that an idea represents an object by *resembling it*, just as a painting of the Eiffel Tower resembles the real Eiffel Tower in some respects, or to use

Locke's own analogy, just as a mirror image resembles the object that it's a reflection of, and thereby represents it.

Berkeley rejects Indirect Realism, or at least the form of it that maintains that we have perceptual access (albeit indirect perceptual access) to material objects out there in the external world. He has a little bit to say about the claim that's at the heart of Inferential Realism – that we can use our faculty of reason to infer the existence and nature of material objects (see, *e.g.*, *Principles* §§18–20; *Dialogues* p. 221). However, it is Representative Realism of the kind commonly attributed to Locke that was 'all the rage' in the seventeenth and eighteenth centuries. This was the theory advocated by many proponents of the 'Corpuscualarian' science of Locke's time, and it's the theory towards which Berkeley directs more of his fire (see below, p. 122–3).

vi. THE DISTINCTION BETWEEN PRIMARY AND SECONDARY QUALITIES

We turn now to one of the most important doctrines of the early Modern period, one which has informed our philosophical and scientific thinking ever since, and which captures the intuition that we still hold today that there's a distinction to be drawn between the way things appear to us to be, and the way they really, ultimately, are. It's known as 'the distinction between Primary and Secondary Qualities', and it's a distinction that all three of the philosophers we've been looking at subscribed to in one form or another – although Locke was the first of them to use the terms 'Primary Quality' and 'Secondary Quality', having borrowed them from his good friend Robert Boyle (of Boyle's Law fame).

According to this doctrine, there's a distinction to be drawn between two different kinds of feature, property or 'quality' that an object like a table or a chair can have. A table, for example, has all manner of different properties or qualities, such as a certain shape and size, a certain colour and perhaps a certain smell. Some of these properties will be ones that belong to its true nature, properties that it really does have in and of itself, regardless of whether or not anyone or anything is interacting with it (say by looking at it) – these are the table's 'Primary Qualities'. There is some variation in the properties that different philosophers count as Primary Qualities, but the usual ones are size, shape, extension in space, and a degree of motion or rest.

Some of the properties that we experience the table to have however *aren't* genuine properties of the table as it is in and of itself. These properties are features, not of the way the table really is independent of us, but of our reactions to the table – these are the table's 'Secondary Qualities'. Following the Way of Ideas, according to which it is ideas that we are aware of in the first instance when we perceive using our senses, philosophers in the seventeenth century typically took what became known as the Secondary Qualities to be nothing other than sensations in our minds, and the standard list includes the colours, smells and tastes that we experience objects to have, the sounds we experience them to make and the degrees of heat or cold that we experience them to possess.

One of the main reasons why people took properties like colour and sound merely to be features of our own perceptual reactions to objects was the phenomenon of 'perceptual relativity'. Take colour as an example – the colour that we experience an object to be will be determined by our perceptual circumstances. One and the same object will appear to be a different colour to people in different locations, or to people whose sense faculties are in different orders of repair. For instance, one and the same cloud might look pinky-purple to an observer on the ground, white to an observer flying past it in an aeroplane and yellow to an observer who is suffering from jaundice. Here, the colour that we experience the cloud to have changes with each set of perceptual circumstances, even if the cloud itself hasn't changed one bit. The conclusion that many philosophers in the seventeenth century drew was that colour therefore couldn't be counted among an object's genuine properties, but was instead simply a feature of the way we happened to perceptually interact with the object in question, and likewise for each of the other 'Secondary Qualities'. (In the section on 'the Argument from Perceptual Relativity' in Chapter 4 we'll see Berkeley adopting and adapting this kind of reasoning for his own purposes.)

It might strike you as odd to hear it said that the world as it really is in and of itself independent of observers has no colour and makes no sound and so on. Don't we in fact define colour in terms of the wavelength of light that objects reflect, and sound in terms of the soundwaves that objects emit? And isn't the fact that an object reflects a certain wavelength of light or emits a soundwave of a certain frequency something that's got nothing whatsoever to do with the perceptual circumstances observers happen to be in, if indeed there are any observers around at all? Surely the fact that an object is disposed to reflect a certain wavelength of light, or at least the fact that its surface molecules are such that it is disposed to do so, is part of the description of the way that object really is, in and of itself, independent of the likes of us?

As it goes though, people who draw the distinction between Primary and Secondary Qualities might well agree that there is indeed a sense in which we can define colour or sound in this kind of way, and likewise for the smell, taste or temperature that an object has. Nonetheless, they would insist that there is a distinction between (for example) colour defined in this way and colour *as we experience it*. Say what you like about the surface molecules of an object, or the wavelength of light that it is typically disposed to reflect as a result, or indeed what happens in the brain as a consequence of red wavelengths of light striking the retina – none of this makes any mention whatsoever of the property we experience an object to have when we look at it and see that it is red. And it's *this* property that the man on the street has in mind when he says that an object is red, and which those who draw the distinction define as a Secondary Quality.

Berkeley himself denied that there was any distinction of this kind to be drawn between the properties that objects really have, in and of themselves, and the properties we experience objects to have that are sensations in the minds of perceivers. For him, *all* of an object's properties are sensations in the minds of perceivers, and there is no such thing as a property that an object has independent of what perceivers experience. And in coming to think this way, Berkeley may well have received a helping hand from Malebranche. Malebranche himself did draw a distinction between the properties of an object that are merely perceptual reactions in us and the genuine properties that an object really does have in and of itself, claiming that the latter are those that God's intellectual idea of the object reveals to us. But he maintained that *all* of the properties that our *senses* tell us about (the 'sensible qualities', as he calls them) are nothing other than sensations (which for Malebranche are 'modifications of the soul'). In doing so, he may well have directly inspired Berkeley to reach the same conclusion.

I'll say something about the arguments Berkeley uses to attempt to establish this in Chapter 4, but for now I'll note that in doing so he's often accused of misunderstanding the distinction between Primary and Secondary Qualities. The reason for this is that *Locke's* standard version of the distinction is subtly different from the one I've outlined above. On occasion, Locke does define Secondary Qualities as sensations. And at other times, he seems to define Secondary Qualities in terms of the Primary Qualities of the microscopic parts of objects that (for example) reflect light in such a way that we are caused to see the colours we do. Most usually though Locke defines Secondary Qualities as *dispositions* that objects have to cause the sensations of colour or sweetness or sound *etc.* that we experience.

We ourselves are used to talking in terms of the various dispositional properties that an object can have. For instance, we might say that a vase has the dispositional property of fragility, in the case that the vase would smash easily if it were struck or if it fell to the ground. And we happily accept that this property of fragility is a genuine property of the vase, which it retains even if the disposition is never *manifested* (*i.e.*, even if the vase never actually happens to smash). Furthermore, we take it that a vase has the dispositional property of fragility in virtue of certain fundamental properties of the vase, such as the strength of the bonds in the vase's underlying molecular structure. In the same way, Locke maintains that Secondary Qualities such as colour are genuine, if *dispositional*, properties of objects, which objects retain even if these dispositions are never manifested (*e.g.*, even if no one ever actually comes into perceptual contact with the objects and consequently experiences the colour sensations *etc.* that they are disposed to produce in us). And just as a vase is fragile in virtue of the strength of the bonds in the vase's underlying molecular structure, so for Locke objects have the Secondary Qualities that they do in virtue of the Primary Qualities (such as the size and shape) of the tiny parts that make up the object.

I'm going to argue later on that it's irrelevant for our purposes whether or not Berkeley misidentified Locke's version of the distinction between Primary and Secondary Qualities (see below, p. 177). I'll come back to this later on though. In the next instance I want to say something more about how Berkeley's predecessors understood ideas and sensations.

vii. IDEAS AND SENSATIONS

It's hopefully clear from what I've said already that *ideas* and *sensations* featured prominently in early Modern philosophy. However, different philosophers sometimes meant different things by these terms, and Berkeley in turn will use them in his own way. I'd like now to look at what Descartes, Malebranche and Locke understood by them in a bit more detail, so that we're better placed to appreciate how Berkeley's thinking compares to that of his predecessors, and indeed to our own.

Today we typically use the term 'idea' to refer, very roughly, to something in our heads that we think about, and we tend to reserve the term for the 'intellectual' thoughts that we have, rather than anything we are aware of when we perceive the world using our senses. (*E.g.*, we might say that we disagree with a political party's ideas, or that someone's solution to a problem is 'a good idea'.) For Berkeley's predecessors though the term had a broader meaning. Descartes, Malebranche and Locke all took ideas to be what we are aware of in the first instance when we think *or* when we perceive using our senses. They also maintained that ideas are essentially *mental* items. This is just to say that ideas have an essential relation to the mind. Without minds there could be no ideas, and consequently ideas are 'mind-dependent', as philosophers put it today. For Descartes and Malebranche, this meant that ideas were also *non-physical*, since they held that physical matter and non-physical minds were two entirely distinct kinds of substance. Locke sits on the fence on this last point though, remaining agnostic on the question of whether or not a purely physical organism might be able to have a mind and to entertain ideas.

We've already seen that Descartes thought that ideas were 'modifications' of the mind or soul – ways that the mind is or manifests itself – and Malebranche agreed with him. In this way, they didn't think that an idea was something extra that existed in addition to the mind. Locke however often talks of ideas as if they were a kind of 'image' which is 'imprinted' on the mind, and which the mind considers from a position of detachment. For him, while ideas are still very much *in* the mind, he seems to take them to be extra things that exist *in addition* to the mind. As we will see, Berkeley would agree with Locke on this point.

Another feature of the account of ideas typically given in the seventeenth and eighteenth centuries was that ideas can never be 'false', as Descartes puts it. By this, he doesn't mean that we can never go wrong in our thinking, or that we can never experience a perceptual illusion or hallucination. Instead, he means that so long as we are paying attention, we can't go wrong when it comes to knowing the contents of our own minds. So, for example, the hallucinating drunk who sees pink elephants *isn't* mistaken in thinking that he has the perceptual idea of some pink elephants (although he would be mistaken in concluding, on the basis of that perceptual idea, that there really are some pink elephants in his proximity). We know fine well when we are having an idea, and what exactly the content of that idea happens to be. Malebranche's way of expressing this thought, which Berkeley would follow, is to say that our ideas are 'perfectly known'.

Descartes and Malebranche, being Rationalists, divided our ideas into two kinds; the ideas we have when we perceive using our senses (which Descartes often calls 'sensations' or 'sensory ideas', and Malebranche calls 'sensations') and the ideas we have when we use our intellect or faculty of reason (which Descartes calls 'intellectual' ideas and Malebranche describes as purely intellectual, non-sensory ideas). Locke meanwhile, being an Empiricist, denied that we could entertain purely intellectual ideas whose content wasn't derived from the ideas we have when we perceive using our senses. Nonetheless, he also divided the ideas that we can have into two broad kinds – 'ideas of sensation' (the basic components of our sensory experiences) and 'ideas of reflection' (through which we are aware of the kinds of thinking we ourselves are capable of). Locke also held that once the mind is stocked with the basic ideas that we get from these two sources, we can then go on to combine and manipulate them in various ways, and in doing so come to entertain ideas of things we never did see (such as a unicorn), and to know things that weren't *directly* recorded in our experiences but which can be worked out from things that were.

All three of them then take 'sensations' to be a subset of ideas; specifically, the ideas we have when we perceive using our senses, and also when we experience feelings like hunger, fear, anger, pleasure and pain. We ourselves today typically reserve the term 'sensation' for certain kinds of feelings we experience, usually (though not exclusively) via the sense of touch, such as a tingling sensation, or the sensation of orgasm. For philosophers in the seventeenth and eighteenth centuries though the term again had a wider reference. They extended it to refer to any kind of first-up experience we might have, such as the experiences we have via our senses of the sound of a trumpet, the taste of a pineapple, the smell of coffee, the visual experience of the colour red, the feel of the texture of velvet or the sight or feeling of the shape of a ball.

With respect to at least some sensations, Descartes, Malebranche and Locke were in agreement that these taken by themselves tell us nothing about the way material objects really are, and are nothing like any of the genuine features of material objects. So, for example, the sensations of colour, smell, taste, sound and warmth/cold (*i.e.*, the Secondary Qualities in the standard, non-Lockean, sense of the term) that we experience when we perceptually interact with material objects are nothing like, and tell us nothing whatsoever about, the actual, genuine features of those material objects. (They sometimes call these properties the 'sensible qualities' – those properties which are proper to, or are purely functions of, our sensory experiences, and which are distinct from the genuine properties that material objects have independent of our perceptual interaction with them).

Descartes and Locke however both thought that certain other sensations we experience when we perceive material objects *can* tell us about what those objects are really like, such as the sensations we have of an object's shape and size. In Descartes' case, when we are thinking carefully these sensations allow us to go on to *infer* what material objects are really like in and of themselves, and we can come to know on this basis, for instance, that a material object really does have the size and shape we perceive it to have. For Locke, sensations such as the ones we have of an object's size and shape can *resemble* the object's actual size and shape, and in this way again we can come to know the object's actual size and shape.

Malebranche though denied that *any* of our sensations can tell us about what material objects are really like. Recall that for him, it's only when we choose to be open to receiving it, by thinking carefully about what we are aware of via our senses, that God shares with us His own intellectual (non-sensory) idea of extended matter. Rather than any of our sensations, it is God's intellectual idea alone that informs us of the way the world really is. Consequently, Malebranche extends the term 'sensible qualities' to cover *all* of the properties of objects that we experience objects to have when we perceive using our senses – these are all sensations, *all* of which are distinct from and tell us nothing about the genuine properties that material objects have independent of our perceptual interaction with them. Again, Berkeley would follow Malebranche in describing *all* of the properties of everyday objects as 'sensible qualities' in this way.

A related point made explicitly by Malebranche is that *all* sensations are *indescribable* – there's no way you can hope to describe in words what the sensation of being in pain is like, or what the sensation you experience when you see the colour red is like, and so on for all the other sensations. And it follows from this that, for Malebranche at least, there's no way we can bring someone to understand what a given sensation is like by describing features of the material world and material objects. In fact, the only way someone can come to know what a given sensation is like is by experiencing the sensation in question.

Locke makes the same kind of point when he states that all

sensations are 'simple ideas'. As such, they don't have any simpler parts in terms of which they can be analysed, described or thought about. So I can't explain to you what a given sensation is like by telling you about its constituent elements – it has none. Instead, as is the case for all 'simple ideas', Locke holds that we can only come to know what a given sensation is like by experiencing it.

To recap then, ideas for many of Berkeley's early Modern predecessors are all kinds of mental things, including what the mind is aware of in the first instance whenever we think and whenever we perceive the world using our senses. They enjoy an essential relation to the mind, either as modifications of the mind, or as something that exists in addition to the mind which the mind considers from a position of detachment, and we can't go wrong when it comes to knowing our own ideas. Sensations meanwhile are (mainly) the ideas we have when we perceive using our senses. At least some of them tell us nothing about the way material objects really are, and are nothing like any of the genuine features of material objects. For at least some early Modern philosophers, sensations were taken to be indescribable in words, and we could only come to know what a given sensation is like by experiencing it.

The thought that what we experience in the first instance when we perceive using our senses are sensations, which are perfectly known yet indescribable, which can only be known by experiencing the sensations in question, and which are nothing like and can tell us nothing about the features of material objects out there beyond our minds, was one that Berkeley would pick up and run with to potentially devastating effect, as we'll soon see.

CHAPTER 3

BERKELEY'S PHILOSOPHICAL SYSTEM: WHAT THERE IS AND HOW WE COME TO KNOW IT

In this chapter we're going to work through the key features of Berkeley's 'positive' philosophy – his own account of what there is in existence and how we come to know the things we do. (We'll encounter his 'negative' philosophy – his attack on what other people had to say – in Chapter 4, when we turn to examine the arguments and other strategies that he employed in his attempt to *prove* that his account was the right one and that his philosophical opponents were mistaken). As I've mentioned previously I'll be restricting my analysis by and large to what Berkeley wrote in his two major philosophical works, the *Principles* and the *Dialogues* – but rather than bombarding you with quotations from the primary texts I'll provide you with page references at various points so that you can look up for yourself the passages where Berkeley deals with the topics we'll be covering.

As well as explaining the central tenets of Berkeley's philosophical system, I'll also introduce some of the questions you can usefully start to consider in the process of working out whether or not you're impressed by what he says. Again, we'll worry about his main attempts to *prove* that he's right in Chapter 4. My primary aim before then is to get you thinking about the *plausibility* (or otherwise) of Berkeley's philosophy (see above, pp. 22–3). Are the various claims he makes about the ultimate nature of reality and our place in it acceptable to us in principle, or are they irretrievably at odds with some of the basic commitments we're not prepared to give up concerning the way things are? Many people think that

Berkeley's account of the world is just plain daft. What we're going to do is take a good look at what he says and ask whether or not it is as daft as all that. When all's said and done, are his views more or less ridiculous than our own?

i. IDEAS, THOUGHTS AND SENSATIONS

Berkeley is going to conclude that immaterialism (the view that there is no such thing as matter) and idealism (the view that everyday objects are collections of ideas in the mind) are true. His path to this conclusion sees him following the 'Way of Ideas', just as Descartes, Malebranche and Locke had done before him (see above, pp. 31 & 39) – like many of his early Modern predecessors, Berkeley takes it to be the case that what we are aware of in the first instance in the process of becoming acquainted with the world around us are our own ideas (*i.e.*, episodes in our own minds) – see, *e.g.*, *Principles* §1; *Dialogues* p. 230. What distinguishes him from his contemporaries though was his own particular analysis of the nature of these ideas, and it's this analysis that led him to the view that there can't possibly be any material objects in existence, and that tables and chairs *etc.*, while undeniably real, can't exist beyond the mind. So let's start by taking a look at how Berkeley defines ideas and what he says about their nature.

Berkeley's use of the term term 'idea'

For Berkeley, ideas constitute one of the two basic kinds of thing that exist, (minds being the other) – see, e.g., *Principles* §89; *Dialogues* p. 235. They are things (or 'substances') in their own right, not features of some more basic or fundamental kind of stuff. Nonetheless, ideas are 'mind-dependent' – they are *mental* items – because they have an essential relation to the mind. If there were no minds in existence then there would be no ideas, and there can't be any such thing as an idea which exists by itself, out of all relation to the mind. But contrary to the picture given to us by Descartes and Malebranche, ideas aren't related to the mind as a mode is to a substance (see above, pp. 42–3 & 49). Ideas for Berkeley aren't ways in which a mind *manifests* itself or something a mind does. Rather, he tells us that ideas are related to a mind as a thing perceived is to a perceiver (see, *e.g.*, *Dialogues* p. 237) – ideas are what we are aware of when we are carrying out certain kinds of mental activity.

Ideas aren't the only kind of mental item the mind can be aware of, however, and here we see Berkeley using the term 'idea' in a more restrictive sense than many of his immediate predecessors did. Descartes, Malebranche and Locke each used the term 'idea' in a broad sense to refer to what we are aware of in the first instance when we think *or* when we perceive using our senses. Berkeley meanwhile typically uses the term in a narrower sense to refer to what we are aware of in the first instance when we perceive using our senses, when we experience 'passions' such as feelings of hunger or anger, or when we use our imaginations to combine the things we've perceived using our senses in new and novel ways (see, *e.g.*, *Principles* §1). He distinguishes ideas from 'thoughts' (or 'notions', to use his term), which are what the mind is aware of in the first instance when it is contemplating items other than ideas.

Berkeley also tells us that ideas are entirely 'passive' (see, *e.g.*, *Principles* §25; *Dialogues* p. 217). By this he means that they don't have any power themselves to change the way anything else is. Ideas just sit there, if you like, under the mind's gaze. In this way, an idea can't be like a mind (which is 'active', and does have the power to change the way other things are), and so we can't have an idea which represents to us, or is 'of', the mind. Passive ideas can't capture the essence of active minds. So for Berkeley, we aren't aware of the mind by having an 'idea' of it – see, *e.g.*, *Principles* §27; *Dialogues* p. 231. (If it sounds odd to say that we can have no idea of the mind, just recall Berkeley's restrictive use of the term 'idea' – ideas are what we are aware of when we perceive using our senses, when we experience feelings like hunger or anger, or when we combine the ideas we get from our senses in new and novel ways. He's simply insisting that we don't come to know about minds via any of these sources. Berkeley *doesn't* deny that we can have a thought or a 'notion' of the mind, however).

Berkeley's use of the term 'sensation'

The ideas we are aware of when we perceive using our senses Berkeley calls 'ideas of sense', and he's even more specific in his definitions here – ideas of sense are all *sensations*. Now, this last fact – that he takes the ideas we are aware of in the first instance in perception to be *sensations* – is all too often overlooked by people who are studying Berkeley. It's commonly thought that his major arguments turn on the more general claim that the things we are aware of when we perceive using our senses are *ideas*, and indeed he certainly does make this claim. However, it's by coming to appreciate that it's specifically *sensations* that he has in mind here that we will be able to see the full force of those arguments.

In claiming that what we're aware of in the first instance when we perceive using our senses are sensations, Berkeley is so far in agreement with Descartes, Malebranche and Locke (see above, pp. 50–2). But it is Berkeley's understanding of the nature of sensations that marks him apart from his predecessors here. He thought, given the nature of sensations, that there were some important consequences that his predecessors had missed – namely that our perceptual ideas can't possibly represent or be ideas *of* material objects out there beyond the mind, and indeed that the very idea of a material object existing beyond the mind doesn't even make sense. We'll be taking a closer look at these last two lines of thought later on in Chapter 4. For now though I just want to reiterate this crucial fact – that for Berkeley, the 'ideas of sense' [those things we are aware of when we perceive using our senses] are *sensations*.

To be fair though, it's not always immediately clear that Berkeley *does* claim that what we are aware of when we perceive using our senses are not just ideas, but are specifically sensations. For one thing he uses a bewildering range of terms for the things that we perceive (including 'sensible things', 'sensible objects', 'ideas of sense', 'sensible impressions' and 'ideas imprinted on the senses', among many others). So too, he sometimes says that the things we perceive are ideas *or* sensations – and this at a first glance is ambiguous. On the face of it this might suggest that he thinks that the things we perceive are *either* ideas on the one hand, *or* sensations on the other, which would leave the door open for some of the things we perceive being ideas which aren't sensations. However, when we pay close attention to what Berkeley says in the *Principles* and the *Dialogues* it becomes clear that when he says that the things we perceive are ideas *or* sensations, he intends 'ideas' and 'sensations' here to be alternative names for one and the same thing because for him sensations are a specific kind of idea. For example, at §18 of the *Principles* he states that by our senses, 'we have the knowledge only of our sensations, ideas or those things that are immediately perceived by sense, *call them what you will*' (my emphasis). And on p. 197 of the *Dialogues* Berkeley makes it quite clear that the things we perceive are sensations, by having Hylas confess to Philonous that 'upon a fair observation of what passes in my mind, I can discover nothing else, but that I am a thinking being, affected with a variety of sensations'.

What we perceive are sensations

So what does Berkeley mean when he says that what we are aware of in the first instance when we perceive using our senses are *sensations*? What does he understand by the term, and what does he say about the nature of sensations? Well, for one thing, as his predecessors in the seventeenth century did before him, he extends the term 'sensation' to cover not just feelings like the tingling sensation of an itch, or the sensation of orgasm, but also the basic conscious experiences we have when we perceive using any of our senses.

Let's take our sense of sight as an example. Berkeley has it that what we are aware of in the first instance when we look around us aren't material objects like tables and chairs. What we're aware of first up is simply an array of colours taking up our field of vision (see, *e.g.*, *Principles* §1; *Dialogues* p. 197). According to Berkeley, sorting the hotchpotch of colours we are aware of into distinct patches of colour of various shapes and sizes, and indeed into representations of discrete objects, is something the mind does automatically and (usually very shortly) *after* it has registered the initial hotchpotch of colour.

But even once our minds have done this, *strictly speaking* all we're aware of in the first instance when we open our eyes are (now neatly organized) patches of colour. Now these patches of colour may well represent to us objects out there in the world around us. Depending on the size and proximity to us of the objects they represent, some of these patches of colour will take up a larger extent in our visual field than others and some of them will have more sharply defined edges than others. And the various patches may well move around in our visual field as the hotchpotch of colours rearranges itself when the objects they represent move about or when we turn our heads *etc.* But when all's said and done, it is patches of colour that we're aware of in the first instance nonetheless.

By way of an analogy here, consider the sense in which what we're given in the first instance with a painting, before we attend to what the painting is of, is simply an array of coloured patches of paint taking up the extent of the canvas. Or consider the sense in which what we're given in the first instance with a television screen, before we attend to what the television picture is of, is merely an array of coloured pixels taking up the extent of the screen. Again certain expanses of paint or certain collections of pixels will take up larger or smaller portions of the canvas or screen, will have more or less sharply defined edges, and in the case of the television screen will be moving about, and in doing so they will represent to us various objects in the world as being a certain shape and size and a certain distance from our vantage point. Be that as it may though, there's still the basic fact that all we're given in the first instance is a hotchpotch of coloured paint or pixels.

Now, what we are aware of when we see a given colour, according to Berkeley, is a *sensation* (see, *e.g.*, *Dialogues* pp. 197 and 201). So it's a green sensation that we're aware of when we see the colour green, and it's a red sensation that we're aware of when we see the colour red. And these sensations belong to the same family as sensations of pain or pleasure – a family of conscious experiences of various kinds which are essentially episodes in our minds that are characterized and defined by the way they feel to us. I'll say some more about Berkeley's understanding of the nature of these and other sensations in just a moment, but for now it's enough to note that he thinks that what we're aware of when we see the arrays of colour that we do when we open our eyes is just a bunch of *sensations* of colour. And hence the distinct patches of colour of various sizes and shapes that we sort this hotchpotch into are just various collections of sensations of colour.

It's a similar story for the other senses too. When we touch, hear, smell or taste something, according to Berkeley, what we're aware of in the first instance once again aren't material objects out there in the world beyond us. Rather, what we're given first up is a hotchpotch of sounds, smells and tastes and 'feels', depending on which sense you're using. ('Feels' here is my term for the basic experiences we're aware of via our sense of touch. Berkeley himself uses terms like 'tangible qualities'). These he takes to be nothing other than sensations – for instance, the sensation of the feel of a warmed eiderdown, the sensation of the sound of a trumpet, the sensation of the smell of freshly ground coffee, or the sensation of the taste of a lemon (see, *e.g.*, *Dialogues* p. 197).

And again, for Berkeley, these sensations are all members of the same family as sensations of pain or pleasure, and as such they are episodes in our minds – conscious experiences of various kinds that are essentially defined by the characteristic and subjective 'feel' that is unique to the experience in question (or by *what it is like* for the individual who is experiencing it to have a particular sensation, as philosophers often put it today. Under this head, philosophers today also often talk of the 'phenomenal' or 'qualitative' properties (or '*qualia*') which are unique to and which characterize a given sensation).

From the general tenor of what he says about them, it's clear that Berkeley understands sensations – including the 'perceptual' sensations – to be conscious experiences of this kind (see, *e.g.*, *Principles* §3; *Dialogues* p. 197). That is, for him, sensations are all conscious experiences which are essentially defined and characterized by what it feels like to have them from the perceiver's subjective perspective. What else does he say about them?

Berkeley's understanding of the nature of sensations

For one thing, like many of his early Modern forebears, Berkeley held that sensations are **mind-dependent** – they are *mental* items – because they too have an essential relation to the mind. We've already seen that, for him, sensations are a species of *idea* – and ideas are uncontroversially mind-dependent or mental items. As Berkeley puts it, an idea's (and hence a sensation's) *esse* is *percipi* – its existence consists in the fact that it is being perceived (by a mind) – see, *e.g.*, *Principles* §3; *Dialogues* p. 230). If there were no minds in existence, there could be no ideas and no sensations. And as conscious experiences of various kinds, the 'perceptual' sensations such as the sensation of the sound of a trumpet can't conceivably exist beyond the mind of a conscious subject any more than a sensation of pain or a feeling of anger can.

Nonetheless, Berkeley insists that sensations are most definitely **real** (see, *e.g.*, *Principles* §90; *Dialogues* p. 249), and by claiming this he perhaps has two things in mind. First, he may well want to steer us away from the temptation to think of the things that exist purely 'in our heads' as being somehow flimsy or insubstantial, to be contrasted with the real things that populate the material world out there beyond our minds. Berkeley of course denies that there is any such thing as a material world out there beyond our minds, and he may have worried that any talk of the contents of our minds (such as our sensations) being anything less than real might risk us continuing to flirt with the kind of philosophical worldview that he was keen to dispel. Secondly, and more concretely, recall that sensations (as a species of idea) form part of one of the two basic kinds of thing or substance that really do exist. By insisting that sensations are real, Berkeley is perhaps drawing our attention to the fact that on his account ideas (and hence sensations) aren't merely *modifications* of minds – ways in which minds exist or manifest themselves. Ideas (and hence sensations) aren't merely features of some more fundamental kind of thing or substance – they are real things in their own right.

Berkeley again follows his predecessors like Descartes and Malebranche when he claims that sensations are '**perfectly known**' (see above, p. 51, and see, *e.g.*, *Principles* §87; *Dialogues* p. 238). Because sensations can't exist beyond our conscious experience of them (since their *esse* is *percipi*), and because we are 'immediately' aware of the sensations we are having (they are directly present to our consciousness), there is no possibility that we can go wrong when it comes to knowing which sensations we are having and what they are like. To give you an example of my own, it wouldn't even really make sense, if you're experiencing a sharp, stabbing tooth-ache, for someone else to say that you're not, or for them to say that in fact you're experiencing a dull, throbbing toothache, *and for that person to be right*. We might of course struggle on occasion to put into words what a given sensation is like, or we might even *misreport* what it is like. So too, Berkeley concedes that we might go wrong in the conclusions that we draw, on the basis of a given sensation, concerning the way the world is (see, *e.g.*, *Dialogues* p. 238). Nonetheless, the point remains that we'll know fine well that we're having the sensation in question and what it feels like to have it.

Related to this last point is Berkeley's claim that all we are aware of in the first instance (or 'immediately' or 'directly') when we experience a given sensation is the sensation in question itself. Here's another example of my own – consider the sensation of the smell of coffee. Berkeley would say that all you're aware of in the first instance when you experience the sensation of the smell of coffee is the sensation of the smell of coffee. You may well come to know in addition, on the basis of this sensation, that there is some coffee in the vicinity, but you only come to know this 'indirectly' – this information isn't directly recorded in the sensation itself (because it's possible to have a sensation of the smell of coffee even if there isn't any coffee in the vicinity). For Berkeley, it's the habitual connection in your experience between the sensation of the smell of coffee and there being some coffee in the vicinity that causes you to go on to *infer* that some coffee is in the vicinity the next time you experience the sensation of the smell of coffee. But all you're *immediately* aware of when you have the sensation of the smell of coffee is the sensation itself. Another way that Berkeley sometimes makes the same point is by saying that **there is no**

distinction to be drawn between a sensation and its 'object' (see, *e.g.*, *Dialogues* pp. 194–5) – that is, between the sensation itself and what it is that the sensation is 'of' or tells you about in the first instance.

Next, we come to the lynch-pin in Berkeley's account of sensations, and indeed one of the most important claims in the whole of his philosophy – **nothing can be like a sensation but a sensation.** (In fact, he often uses the more general phrase 'nothing can be like an idea but an idea', but it's clear in context when he says this that he intends the claim to apply generally to ideas and specifically to sensations – see, *e.g.*, *Principles* §90; *Dialogues* p. 206). Take again my example of the sensation of pain you have when you've got a toothache. It doesn't really seem to even make any sense to suggest that there could be anything like the pain that you feel out there in the external world, beyond the minds and conscious experiences of those who can feel pain. Berkeley simply extends this kind of thinking to all of our sensations – there can be nothing like the sensation we have when we see the colour red, or hear the sound of a trumpet, or enjoy the taste of a lemon *etc.* out there in the external world, beyond our minds.

In fact Berkeley makes the more specific claim that nothing can be like a sensation of *a given kind* but a sensation *of the same kind*. For one thing, he tells us that **the sensations proper to each of our five senses are 'heterogeneous'** (that is, they are completely different kinds of sensation – see, *e.g.*, *Principles* §44; *Dialogues* p. 206). By this, he means that the sensations we get via the sense of sight are nothing like the sensations we get via the other senses, and likewise for the sensations we get via the senses of touch, hearing, smell and taste. Berkeley would insist that the sensation of the colour red, for example, is nothing like the sensation of the sound of a trumpet (contrary to what some people say). While we might use the same words like 'bright' or 'vibrant' to describe each of these sensations, the basic experience we have when we see the colour red is not a bit like the basic experience we have when we hear the sound of a trumpet. The two sensations are of a completely different order and have completely different characters from one another.

So, for Berkeley, neither our sensations themselves (since they are mind-dependent conscious experiences), nor the things our sensations are sensations 'of' in the first instance (since there is no distinction to be drawn between a sensation and its 'object'), nor anything like our sensations (since nothing can be like a sensation but a sensation) can exist beyond the mind.

Of course we ourselves take it that there are many things 'beyond the mind' involved in the *process* that brings us to experience the sensations that we do. But Berkeley's present point is just that none of these things can be anything like our sensations themselves. For instance, when we see the colour red it may well be the case that this is because an object (say a strawberry) has surface molecules which reflect a red wavelength of light, which in turn on striking our retinas activates certain rods and cones in our eyes, thus causing electrical information to be sent along our optic nerves into our brains *etc*. Be that as it may, Berkeley would insist that we're aware of no part of this process in the first instance when we have a red sensation, bar the sensation itself that's the end result – and no part of this process bar the sensation itself is anything like the sensation we are aware of when we see the colour red. And it's this kind of thing that he has in mind when he says that nothing can be like a sensation but a sensation.

Now since he takes sensations to be conscious experiences in our minds, and since he takes it to be the case that nothing can be like a sensation but a sensation, Berkeley also holds that **we can only come to any sort of conception, and on that basis knowledge, of what a given sensation is like by having a conscious experience of the relevant kind** – *i.e.*, by having the sensation in question. (Berkeley explicitly spells out this line of thought most fully in his *Theory of Vision . . . Vindicated and Explained* – for further details of this book see above, p. 11). What he means by this is that you can only know what (for instance) people see when they see the colour red if you've seen that colour yourself. And you can only hope to possess an adequate concept of the colour red if you've seen that colour yourself. Here, Berkeley himself gives us the example of a man who's been blind since birth – such a man he says can't possibly hope to understand what the colour red is, or any other colour for that matter, because such a man simply hasn't had the relevant conscious experiences (see, *e.g.*, *Principles* §77).

And a further point related to this last thought that Berkeley would subscribe to is that **it is impossible to adequately describe a sensation and what it is like in objective, third-person terms**. (In fact Berkeley doesn't explicitly say this, but it follows nonetheless from his account of the nature of sensations. So too, it was a tenet that was commonly held in his day – see above, pp. 53–4). In the case of the sensation of the colour red for example, no amount of scientific explanation in terms of the properties of light or of the surface molecules of light-reflecting objects and so on will capture the defining essence of the sensation of the colour red. Instead, we can only properly explain or describe a given sensation and what it is like with reference to a first-person, subjective conscious experience of the right kind. For instance, someone might describe to you the sensation they get from time to time as a result of an old eye injury by comparing it to the sensation you get when you poke a finger in your eye. But if you've never had *that* sensation – if you don't know what that particular first-person, subjective experience is like – this description will probably be meaningless to you.

Again, Berkeley's claim that all we are aware of in the first instance when we perceive using our senses are sensations lies right at the heart of his philosophy, and I'll suggest ways in which you might start think about whether he's right about this in Chapter 4 (see below, pp. 126–9). So too, I'll be recalling various aspects of his understanding of the nature of sensations in fleshing out and initially defending some of his arguments for immaterialism and idealism that we'll also encounter in Chapter 4. For now though, having seen Berkeley's understanding of the term 'sensation', we are in a position to move on to look in closer detail at the kinds of things which Berkeley took to be nothing other than sensations or collections of sensations, and how we go about perceiving them.

ii. EVERYDAY OBJECTS, THEIR PROPERTIES AND HOW WE PERCEIVE THEM

Berkeley is an idealist – he claims that everyday objects, like tables and chairs, are ideas in our minds. Indeed, he tells us that each object that populates the world out there is in fact a *collection* of ideas, or more specifically a collection of sensations (see, *e.g.*, *Principles* §1; *Dialogues* p. 249). From gnats to elephants, from tables to chairs and from the moons of Jupiter to our own bodies, eyes and brains – all of these things are nothing other than collections of the sensations that are our ideas of sense. And because sensations are mind-dependent (see above, p. 62), so too are the everyday objects that they make up – objects like elephants or bananas or ears are all *mental items*. They have an essential relation to the mind – if there were no minds in existence, there would be no such objects; and there can't be any such thing as an elephant, banana or ear which exists by itself, out of all relation to the mind.

But what *precisely* does Berkeley mean when he says that everyday objects are collections of sensations? To use his own example from the very first section of the main body of the *Principles*, an apple is made up of the sensations we have when we see the array of colours that constitutes the way the apple looks, when we experience the taste or smell of an apple, when we experience the 'feels' that we do when we touch an apple, as so on. Because we experience these various sensations to go together, we consider them to be a single object. And as Berkeley makes clear in his *New Theory of Vision* (for further details of this book see above, pp. 9–11), grouping the various sensations we have into objects in this way is the business of the early stages of our development, and it is the *habitual* experience we have of the sensations that make up a given object continually going together that is doing the driving here. We come to learn that the visual sensations that constitute the look of an apple are often accompanied by the 'gustatory' sensation of the taste of an apple, and 'tactual' sensation of the 'feel' of an apple, and so on – and this is what a given apple is: this particular taste plus this particular look plus this particular 'feel' *etc*.

So too for Berkeley, the various properties or qualities that objects have, such as their colour, size and shape, are all sensations (see, *e.g.*, *Principles* §99; *Dialogues* p. 249). In fact, these properties are the sensations which make up the collection that constitute the object of which they are the properties. An object's colour *is* the set of visual sensations we have when we look at it; its smell *is* the 'olfactory' sensation we have when we inhale through our noses in its proximity; its temperature and texture are among the sensations we have for example when we run our hands over it; and its taste *is* the gustatory sensation we have when we explore it with our tongues.

An object's size and shape too are just features or functions of the sensations that we have (see, *e.g.*, *Principles* §§5 and 87), and as it happens Berkeley distinguishes between an object's *visible* size and shape and its *tangible* size and shape – that is, its size and shape as revealed by our sense of touch. (He makes this distinction explicit in his *New Theory of Vision* and *Theory of Vision . . . Vindicated and Explained*). An object's visible size and shape are just the shape and size of the particular expanse of colour that constitutes the look of the object, while its tangible size and shape are just the size and shape of the particular expanse of 'feels' that we experience, for example when we run our hands over the object. And of course an expanse of colour is nothing like an expanse of 'feels'. Now, we typically think that we can perceive an object's size and shape by both sight and touch, and that it's one and the same size and shape that we experience in each case. But Berkeley denies that this is so – an object's visible size and shape simply aren't the kinds of thing we can perceive by touch, because its visible size and shape are features unique to expanses of sensations of colour, and we can't perceive expanses of sensations of colour using our hands. Likewise, its tangible size and shape aren't the kinds of thing we can perceive by sight – they are features unique to expanses of 'feels', and we can't perceive expanses of 'feels' by sight. According to Berkeley, we speak very loosely when we say that we perceive one and the same size and shape by both sight and touch. The only reason we do speak in this way, he thinks, is that we're simply used to experiencing the sensations that constitute an object's visible size and shape and the sensations that constitute its tangible size and shape at (approximately) the same time, and so for our own convenience we use the same words to refer to both sets of sensations. (Again Berkeley spells this out in his *Theory of Vision . . . Vindicated and Explained.*)

Next, in maintaining that *all* of an object's properties are sensations or composites of sensations, Berkeley rejects the traditional distinction between Primary and Secondary Qualities, according to which some of the properties objects have are nothing more than sensations in our minds (the Secondary Qualities) while others aren't (the Primary Qualities) – see above, pp. 46–50, and see, *e.g.*, *Principles* §§9–10; *Dialogues* pp. 187–8. For him, *all* of an object's properties are sensations in our minds, and we'll see how he tries to argue for this claim in Chapter 4.

So too, note how the relationship between an object and its properties on Berkeley's account isn't like that between a pincushion and its pins – the Aristotelian account – or between a substance and its modes – the Cartesian account – (see above, pp. 42–3), but is the relationship of a whole to its parts. An everyday object for Berkeley is a collection of sensations, and the sensations that make up the collection are the properties of the object in question.

Recall too that, for Berkeley, ideas (including sensations) can exist only insofar as they are perceived – that is, only insofar as a mind is aware of them or is 'having' them (see above, p. 62). Now because everyday objects like tables and chairs are collections of ideas (and specifically sensations), tables and chairs likewise can only exist insofar as they are perceived – that is, insofar as a mind is aware of or 'has' the ideas that make them up. As Berkeley puts it, for everyday objects and their properties, as for ideas, their existence consists in the fact that they are being perceived – their *esse* is *percipi* (see, *e.g.*, *Principles* §3; *Dialogues* pp. 230 and 234). Indeed, this claim – that for ideas/sensations and for everyday objects and their properties, their *esse* is *percipi* – has become the watchword or slogan for Berkeley's philosophy, and is sometimes referred to as his '*esse* is *percipi*' principle or '*esse* is *percipi*' thesis. (Make sure that you don't call it his '*esse est percipi*' principle though, or some Berkeley scholars will get very upset, because Berkeley himself never used the Latin word for 'is' in this particular context). Consequently, the very thought of an idea or everyday object existing that isn't being perceived by some mind or other (or that some mind or other isn't aware of) is a complete nonsense for Berkeley. There can be no 'mind-independent' ideas or objects – ideas or objects which exist by themselves, out of all relation to the mind – in this way.

Berkeley's theory of perception – immediate vs. mediate perception

This picture in hand, let's flesh out Berkeley's account of how it is that we perceive everyday objects using our senses and indeed his general theory of sense perception. We've seen how he claims that what we're aware of in the first instance (or 'immediately' or 'directly') when we perceive using any one of our senses are the sensations that the sense faculty in question is uniquely geared to provide us with (*e.g.*, sensations of colour for sight, 'feels' for touch, sounds for hearing *etc.*). In the next place, Berkeley goes on to draw a distinction between what we perceive 'immediately' (or 'directly') in this way, and what we perceive 'mediately' (or 'indirectly').

We immediately or directly perceive only those sensations that we are aware of in the first instance *right now*. For example, what I immediately perceive when I open my eyes is the array of sensations of colour that I'm aware of first up, nothing more, nothing less. Likewise, by touch I immediately perceive nothing more than the arrays of tactual sensations (or 'feels') that I'm aware of in the first instance for example when I run my hands over something. So too, we immediately perceive only auditory sensations (sounds) via our sense of hearing, olfactory sensations (smells) via our sense of smell, and gustatory sensations (tastes) via our sense of taste.

As for the things we mediately or indirectly perceive, Berkeley claims that, on perceiving the sensations that we're immediately or directly aware of right now, our minds can automatically recall various other sensations that we've experienced previously (see, *e.g.*, *Principles* §33; *Dialogues* p. 204). Specifically, our minds can automatically recall other sensations which we've learned to *associate* with the sensations we're immediately perceiving right now, on the basis of the fact that we've regularly experienced them to go together in the past. For example, in the past I've regularly experienced the sight of an apple and the taste of an apple to go together, and as a result, the next time I immediately perceive the array of sensations of colour that make up the sight of an apple, my mind can automatically jump to the thought of the taste of an apple. Berkeley calls this process 'suggestion', and it's the process by which I can come to mediately or indirectly perceive things other than the sensations I'm immediately perceiving right now (see, *e.g.*, *Principles* §43; *Dialogues* p. 204).

Crucially, this process of suggestion can only bring us to mediately or indirectly perceive sensations that we've immediately perceived at some time or other previously. What we're doing when we mediately perceive something is remembering or recalling past sensations. Berkeley calls these recalled sensations 'ideas of the imagination', because we're aware of them in our 'imaginations'. Be careful here though – by 'imagination' he doesn't mean what we mean by the term today. For Berkeley, as for many other early Modern philosophers, the imagination is the faculty of the mind we're using when we are quite literally aware of 'images'. By 'images' he means the ideas we are aware of in the first instance when we perceive using our senses, the ideas we can recall to mind when we remember the perceptual ideas we've previously had, and the new ideas we can fashion in our minds when we combine the perceptual ideas we've previously had (for instance when we combine the idea of the torso of a horse with the idea of the upper-body of a man to create the idea of a centaur). Again, though, by 'images' Berkeley and his predecessors don't just mean visual pictures. Images include far more than the ideas (or 'visual images') we derive from the sense of sight – they also include the ideas we derive from our other senses too. So, for example, what we are aware of in the first instance when hear something, or remember hearing something, is an auditory image (*i.e.*, an auditory sensation).

Berkeley is quite adamant that these 'ideas of the imagination' which we have when we recall past sensations (*i.e.*, the things we mediately or indirectly perceive) must themselves be sensations – for him these ideas of the imagination copy or 'resemble' our past sensations, and as we've already seen he maintains that 'nothing can be like a sensation but a sensation' (see above, p. 64). If you like, think of the ideas that we have when we remember past sensations as pale or watered-down versions of the original conscious experiences in question.

And the fact that Berkeley takes the things we mediately or indirectly perceive to be sensations is important, because he also says that we can mediately perceive everyday objects like tables and chairs on the basis of the sensations that we immediately perceive right now. (To use one of his own examples (see *Dialogues* p. 204), when I hear the unmistakable sound of a stagecoach, all I immediately perceive is the sound itself, nothing more, nothing less. Nonetheless, this auditory sensation brings my mind to an awareness of the stagecoach itself, given the connection in my past experience between a stagecoach and the sound it makes).

Indeed in a sense, it's Berkeley's assertion that the things we mediately or indirectly perceive are sensations that grounds his jump from his claim that what we're aware of in the first instance (or 'immediately') in perception are sensations to his further claim that everyday objects are (collections of) sensations. We could couch his thinking here in an argument as follows (although Berkeley's own way of putting it isn't so explicitly straightforward) – the things we mediately or indirectly perceive are sensations; we mediately perceive everyday objects like tables and chairs; so everyday objects like tables and chairs are nothing other than (collections of) sensations.

In fact, what happens when I mediately or indirectly perceive an everyday object is that the sensations that I immediately perceive right now, such as the auditory sensations of the sound of a stagecoach, bring my mind to recall other sensations, such as the sensations of colour that make up the look of a stagecoach. And it's these other sensations that we can mediately or indirectly perceive, *along with* the sensations that we immediately perceive right now, which constitute the stagecoach. I don't immediately perceive the coach itself when I hear the sound it makes. All I'm immediately aware of in the first instance here are certain auditory sensations; but of course there's more to the coach on Berkeley's account than just the auditory sensations that comprise the sound it makes – the coach is the combination of the sound it makes, the way it looks, how it feels *etc.* Nonetheless, it's on the basis of the coach's sound that I am immediately aware of right now that I'm brought to recall other sensations from the collection that constitutes the coach, and it's in this way that I come to (mediately or indirectly) perceive the coach itself.

So we can see here that there's a sense in which Berkeley, like many of his immediate predecessors, provides us with an 'indirect' theory of sense perception, according to which everyday objects are something we come to know about indirectly, on the basis of the things we aware of directly or in the first instance when we perceive using our senses (see above, pp. 44–6). But unlike Descartes, Malebranche and Locke, Berkeley denies that the objects we perceive indirectly are material objects out there in the mind-independent realm – rather, they are collections of sensations, some of which aren't among the sensations that we're *immediately* aware of right this second when we perceive using our senses.

To summarize, what we're aware of in the first instance (what we perceive 'immediately' or 'directly') when we perceive with any one of our senses are the sensations which that sense faculty is uniquely geared to provide us with – sensations of colour for sight, 'feels' for touch *etc.* But in sense perception we can also be aware of (*i.e.*, we can mediately or indirectly perceive) sensations *other* than the ones we're immediately perceiving right now, via the process of *suggestion* – namely, sensations which are copies of sensations that we've had previously. Everyday objects like tables and chairs are collections of sensations, some of which we are *immediately* aware of right now, and some of which can be suggested to our minds by the sensations we're immediately aware of right now. And because perceiving an everyday object like a table or a chair involves us recalling to mind (*i.e.*, mediately perceiving) certain sensations that we're not immediately perceiving right now, Berkeley's standard story is that these everyday objects themselves are mediately or indirectly perceived. Simple, huh? Well now it's time to really confuse matters.

An aside – 'strictly speaking' only immediate perception counts as perception proper?

Sometimes we find Berkeley claiming that 'strictly' or 'properly' speaking, we can only perceive the things we immediately or directly perceive, and that we don't *really* or *genuinely* perceive the things we mediately or indirectly perceive (see, *e.g.*, *Dialogues* pp. 203–4). For instance, with his example of the stagecoach that we mediately perceive, he tells us that 'the coach is not [. . .] properly perceived by sense, but suggested from experience', and that we are just talking loosely (*i.e.* non-strictly) when we say that we perceive the coach here. This might strike you as odd. Surely, we would want to say that we *do* perceive the coach with our senses when we hear the sound that it makes?

In fact, there's nothing for us to worry about here. All Berkeley means when he says that 'strictly speaking' we don't perceive the coach is that the coach itself, in its totality, isn't to be found among the things we are *directly* aware of *right this second* when we hear, see and touch the things we do *etc*. In his own example, all we are directly aware of in the first instance when we hear a coach is the sound of the coach – not the coach itself, because there's more to the coach on his account than just the sound it makes.

So when he is speaking 'strictly', Berkeley wants to reserve the term 'perception' to refer to *immediate* perception – the activity wherein we come to be aware of the sensations our senses directly give us right this second. Consequently, when he says that 'strictly speaking' we don't perceive the coach, he just means that we don't immediately or directly perceive it. At other times he is happy to use the term 'perception' in a broader, looser sense, to refer not only to immediate perception, but also to mediate perception – the activity wherein we come to be aware of sensations *other* than the ones we're directly given by our senses right this second (see, *e.g.*, *Dialogues* pp. 204–5 and 255). Here, we also come to perceive (albeit *indirectly*, or *loosely speaking*) other sensations that we recall to mind on the basis of the ones our senses directly give us right now. In conclusion, even though he says that strictly speaking we don't perceive the coach, all he means here is that we don't immediately perceive it. He still allows that we *do* perceive the coach with our senses when we hear the sound that it makes; it's just that we perceive it mediately or indirectly.

Another aside – everyday objects are immediately perceived?

What I've given you above is Berkeley's standard story, according to which everyday objects like tables and chairs are mediately or indirectly perceived. But rather confusingly, Berkeley *sometimes* says that everyday objects like tables and chairs are in fact *immediately* perceived, and on occasion he's very insistent on this point (see, *e.g.*, *Principles* §38; *Dialogues* p. 230). So at first it can look as though Berkeley is being somewhat inconsistent – telling us now that objects like tables and chairs are immediately perceived, and now that they are mediately perceived. Which is it to be? There are in fact a couple of main ways we can resolve this inconsistency – one which Berkeley himself doesn't use, and one which he does.

The one he doesn't use is this. We've seen how for Berkeley everyday objects are collections of sensations, some of which we're immediately aware of right now, and some of which can be suggested to us by the ones we're immediately aware of right now. In which case, we can be said to immediately perceive everyday objects like tables and chairs in the sense that the sensations we are immediately aware of right now are some of their *parts*. As an analogy, consider the way that we ourselves say that we can see a house when in fact perhaps all we can directly see right now are the surfaces of some of the bricks that make up one of its walls, Berkeley could say that we immediately perceive a house by sight in the sense that we are immediately aware of the sensations of colour that make up part of the collection of sensations that is the house. In both cases, what we're *really* aware of in the first instance (or what we perceive 'strictly speaking') are merely *parts* of the object in question. The other parts of the house we're *not* immediately aware of in the first instance, so we don't immediately perceive the *whole* house in its entirety. It's via mediate perception that we can be said to perceive the whole house in its entirety, because it's via mediate perception that we come to be aware of the parts of the house that we're not immediately aware of right now, and it's in this sense that Berkeley can maintain that everyday objects are mediately perceived. Viewed this way, Berkeley isn't in fact being inconsistent when he says on the one hand that everyday objects are immediately perceived, and on the other hand that they are mediately perceived. Here, they are immediately perceived in the sense that we are immediately aware of some of their parts, and they are mediately perceived in the sense that it is only via the process of suggestion that we come to perceive the other parts that make up the collection of sensations that constitute the object in question.

The other way we can resolve this apparent inconsistency, which is based on what Berkeley actually does say, is as follows. There are a number of passages which strongly imply that what Berkeley *sometimes* means when he says that a sensation is 'immediately perceived' is that we have immediately perceived it *at some time or other*, even if we're not immediately perceiving it right this second (see, *e.g.*, *Dialogues* p. 230). And for him, as we've seen, what we mediately perceive (*i.e.*, what is suggested to us on the basis of what we're immediately perceiving right now) are (copies of) sensations that we've immediately perceived at some point in the past. In this way, Berkeley can say that everyday objects like tables and chairs are immediately perceived in the sense that these objects are collections of sensations that we are immediately perceiving right now and/or that we have immediately perceived at some time previously.

What he is doing in effect here is claiming that 'strictly speaking', the only things that we immediately perceive are those sensations that we are immediately aware of right this second. Meanwhile, everyday objects are mediately perceived, yet we might also say ('loosely speaking') that they are immediately perceived, in the sense that they are collections of sensations which we immediate perceive at some time or other.

Berkeley's account of object identity – how different people see the same thing etc

These two caveats aside, I want you to briefly consider a particular puzzle that's generated by Berkeley's account of sense perception – one which he anticipated and responded to himself. Given that an everyday object is supposed to be a collection of ideas, how can different people all be said to perceive one and the same thing? And how can one person be said to perceive one and the same object on different occasions or in different perceptual circumstances? You and I are each aware of *different* sets of ideas when we each perceive a given object – the ideas that I'm aware of are in my head, whereas the ideas that you're aware of are in yours. So how can we both be said to perceive one and the same thing after all? So too, I have one set of perceptual ideas when I look at an object under a microscope and a different set of perceptual ideas when I look at it with the naked eye. Indeed, I have one set of perceptual sensations when I *look* at an object (namely *visual* sensations) and a different set of perceptual sensations when I *touch* it (namely *tactual* sensations). In which case, how can I be said to perceive one and the same thing on each occasion? We ourselves are committed to the view that different people *can* all perceive one and the same thing, and that I can perceive one and the same object in differing perceptual circumstances or via different senses. If Berkeley's philosophy prevents us from holding this view, then that's so much the worse for him, isn't it? In a nutshell, what we're asking here is whether or not Berkeley can provide us with a plausible account of 'object identity'.

In fact Berkeley sometimes says that one and the same object does *not* survive in each of these circumstances. For instance, he tells us that 'strictly speaking' we don't perceive the same objects by sight as we do by touch, and that we don't see one and the same object under the microscope as we do with the naked eye (see, *e.g.*, *Dialogues* p. 245). But what he means by the word 'object' in these cases *isn't* an everyday object like a table or a chair. Instead, he's using the word in this context to refer to whatever it is that we're aware of *in the first instance* when we perceive using our sense of sight or our sense of touch, and what we're aware of *in the first instance* when we look down a microscope or when we look at something with the naked eye. As we've already seen, what he thinks we're aware of in the first instance when we look at something is an array of colours, and what we're aware of in the first instance when we touch something is an array of 'feels'. Hence Berkeley's claim that 'strictly speaking' we can't perceive one and the same object by sight and by touch amounts to nothing more than the pretty obvious claim that we can't directly feel colours or see 'feels'. Likewise, we don't see one and the same object with the naked eye as we do under the microscope because in this case it's a *different* array of colours that we see each time. All that Berkeley is doing when he claims that 'strictly speaking' we don't perceive one and the same object by sight and by touch, or that we don't perceive one and the same object with the naked eye as we do under a microscope, is using the word 'object' in an unusual way (which perhaps he doesn't flag clearly enough) – to refer to whatever it is that we are aware of *in the first instance* in perception.

Indeed on other occasions, Berkeley happily allows that different people can perceive one and the same (everyday) object, and that a single person can perceive one and the same (everyday) object in different perceptual circumstances or via different senses (see, *e.g.*, *Dialogues* pp. 245–8). Again we've already seen how he distinguishes between the things that we immediately or directly perceive and the things that we mediately or indirectly perceive, and that his standard story is that everyday objects like tables and chairs are things that we mediately perceive. And while 'strictly speaking' we don't perceive one and the same object by sight and by touch (in the sense that we immediately see colours and touch 'feels'), we can mediately or indirectly perceive one and the object here.

Recall that, for Berkeley, an everyday object such as an apple is a collection of ideas, some of which I may be immediately perceiving right now, and others of which I won't be. So the apple itself is more than those ideas which I am immediately perceiving right now – it's more than just a particular array of colours, or a particular array of 'feels', for example. To say in truth that I'm perceiving an apple, over and above (for example) just the array of colours that constitutes the look of the apple, I need to bring to mind other ideas from the collection that constitutes the apple, which is what happens in mediate perception. When I immediately perceive part of the collection of ideas that constitutes an apple (such as the array of colours that constitutes the look of the apple), my mind will automatically recall other parts of this collection (such as the gustatory sensations that constitute the taste of the apple), on the basis of the habitual connection in my past experience between the ideas I'm immediately perceiving and the ideas I'm recalling.

Berkeley is then able to say that I can perceive one and the same object by sight and by touch because the ideas I'm immediately aware of in the first instance in each case all belong to the one self-same collection of sensations that constitutes the object in question. It's one and the same object that I *mediately* or *indirectly* perceive in each case, because it's further sensations from one and the same collection of ideas that I recall to mind on the basis of what I see and feel in the first instance when I perceive the object via these different senses.

In a similar fashion, both you and I can perceive one and the same object, because the ideas in my head and the ideas in your head, while comprising two distinct sets of ideas, all belong to the one self-same collection of sensations that constitutes the object in question. We both *mediately* or *indirectly* perceive the same object, because we each recall further sensations from one and the same collection of ideas, on the basis of the ideas that we each immediately perceive in the first instance.

And again I see the same object under a microscope as I do with the naked eye because the visual sensations I have in each case all belong to the one self-same collection of ideas that constitutes the object in question. I *mediately* or *indirectly* perceive the same object in each case, because on both occasions I recall further sensations from one and the same collection of ideas, on the basis of the visual sensations that I'm immediately aware of.

So that's the standard story that Berkeley gives under each of these heads. He does after all give us the means to say that different people can perceive one and the same object, or that I can perceive one and the same object by sight and by touch *etc*. The key to understanding his account here is that, for him, an everyday object such as an apple is more than just a collection of the ideas that an *individual* perceiver has or could have on a *single* occasion. Rather, it is a collection of the ideas that *multiple* perceivers have or could have on *different* occasions. It's in this way, for example, that different people can be said to perceive one and the same everyday object, despite the fact that the ideas in my head are mine and the ideas in your head are yours. It's because we can each have ideas which are (different) parts of one and the same collection of ideas that we can all be said to perceive one and the same thing.

The sense in which we can perceive whole objects

But here's something else for you to think about. We've just noted that the collection of ideas that constitutes a single object is going to include the ideas that *multiple* perceivers have or could have on *different* occasions. Now that's going to be a pretty big collection of ideas, and one consequence of this is that it's going to be impossible for a single person to be aware of all of the ideas that make up the collection that constitutes an object. When I'm looking at an apple, for example, I am immediately or directly aware of the sensations of colour that make up the look of the apple *from my perspective*. And I may be mediately or indirectly aware of *some* of the other sensations from the collection that makes up the apple, such as (a copy of) the sensation of the taste of the apple that my visual sensations suggest to me. But there are plenty of other sensations from the collection which I won't be aware of when I'm looking at the apple, such as the visual sensations that make up the look of the apple from someone else's perspective.

In which case, I can't ever be said to perceive a *whole* object on Berkeley's account, can I, because I can never be aware at any one time of the entire collection of ideas which constitutes the object in question? Given that *we* typically think that we can and do perceive whole objects, should we not reject Berkeley's account of sense perception as implausible? Well, maybe not.

For one thing, Berkeley's account here is perhaps no more implausible under this head than the main rival account of perception held by many of his immediate predecessors. According to Representative Realism, we indirectly perceive material objects by directly perceiving ideas which represent (by resembling) certain properties or features that these material objects really do have out there in the world beyond us (see above, p. 45). But of course on this account we don't directly perceive ideas which represent *all* of a given object's properties or features, and consequently not all of an object's properties or features are recorded in our perceptual experiences at a given time. So there's a sense in which we don't perceive objects in their entirety on the Representative Realist account of perception either.

And perhaps Berkeley's account is in fact no less implausible than *our own* common-sense view here. We don't think that we perceive *all* of an object's features or properties when we look at it or touch it. For instance, when we are looking at a house, we can only see the parts of the outside of the house that are facing us. We don't *literally* see the other side of the house, or the inside of the house. So again, there's a sense in which we don't perceive objects in their entirety on our *own* account of perception. In which case, would it not be unfair of us to complain that this is also the case on Berkeley's account?

In fact there's another sense in which we *do* perceive objects in their entirety on both our own account and on the Representative Realist account of perception: we are in perceptual contact with whole objects *in virtue* of the fact that we are aware in perception of *some* of their properties or features. So, for example, on our own account, we can be said to see the house itself precisely because we can see the parts of the house that we do. But surely the same is true on Berkeley's account of perception – we can be said to perceive the apple itself precisely because we immediately perceive the sensations of colour that are parts of the collection of sensations that constitutes the apple. The fact that we aren't aware of all of the sensations in the collection at any one time is no more damaging to Berkeley's account of perception than the fact that we can't see all of the features of a house at any one time is to our own. My suggestion here then is that Berkeley's account of perception is no more implausible under this head than its rivals.

Berkeley's Empiricism in action

What we've seen with Berkeley's theory of perception is his Empiricism at work (see above, pp. 27–8). He's told us that it is only through having experiences of the right kinds, and more specifically *sensations* of the right kinds, that we can become aware of and hence come to know the things we do about the everyday objects in the world around us. It's through those experiences, and specifically those sensations, that we come to know everything we do about objects like tables, chairs, houses, planets, human bodies *etc*. For Berkeley, we don't have anything akin to the innate ideas which Descartes claimed God created us with the capacity to generate and through which we can come to know about the way things are (see above, pp. 30–1).

That said, there are some other things in existence, aside from our sensations and the everyday objects that they make up, which we don't come to know about directly via *sense* experience (*i.e.*, purely by perceiving the world using our senses). It's time to move on to see what else Berkeley thinks there is in existence aside from our ideas and the objects they comprise.

iii. MINDS (a.k.a. 'SPIRITS')

We've seen that, according to Berkeley, ideas are one of the two basic kinds of thing (or 'substance') in existence. The other is minds (or 'spirits' as he sometimes calls them). For him, as for Descartes previously, there are very many minds in existence. Our minds aren't part of some larger mind or universal consciousness or what have you. We have one mind each, as do the angels (and together with the angels we are 'finite minds' or 'created minds'), and indeed so does God (the 'infinite mind').

I remarked above that Berkeley claims that ideas are entirely 'passive' – they just sit there under the mind's gaze, and they don't have any power themselves to change the way anything else is. Minds however are active – they don't just sit there, they constantly *do* things, and they can change the way that other things are (see, *e.g.*, *Principles* §2; *Dialogues* p. 231). Indeed, minds are *characterized* by the fact that they are active – being active is their defining feature, and they are the only things in existence that are active. For one thing, unlike ideas whose *esse* is *percipi*, the existence of a mind consists in the activity of perceiving (or being aware of or 'having') ideas and thoughts. To use Berkeley's Latin phrase (which he employs elsewhere, in writings other than the *Principles* or the *Dialogues*), for a mind its *esse* is *percipere* – its existence consists in its perceiving activity (see, *e.g.*, *Principles* §139). And this doctrine itself has an interesting entailment for Berkeley. Just as he took it to follow from the claim that the existence of an idea consists in its being perceived that an unperceived idea cannot exist, so he takes it to follow from the claim that the existence of a mind consists in its doing some perceiving (*i.e.*, having thoughts or ideas) that a mind which isn't perceiving doesn't exist either. Hence he claims that the mind must always be thinking – there can't be a time when my mind is genuinely blank or empty. It is always thinking (by perceiving ideas or having thoughts), otherwise it simply wouldn't exist.

As I've already intimated, another way in which minds are active on Berkeley's account consists in their ability to change the way other things are. With respect to human minds, this ability manifests itself in two ways. First, we can *will* certain ideas and thoughts to pop into existence (see, *e.g.*, *Principles* §28). For instance, we can choose to recall various sensations that we've had in the past, and to combine them in interesting new ways, like we do when we summon up an idea of a centaur in our 'mind's eye', by recalling and combining the perceptual ideas we've experienced previously of the torso of a horse and the upper-body of a man. Secondly, we can exercise our wills by choosing to navigate our environments in various ways, and in doing so indirectly bring it about that we experience the fresh sets of sensations that we do (see, *e.g.*, *Dialogues* p. 237). As an example here, suppose I am looking at my computer screen, and perceiving the sensations which constitute it. I can then choose to turn my head and look out of the window, and everything else being equal I will experience a new set of sensations which constitute the field or the tree or the cars or whatever it is that I see when I look out the window. We'll see in a moment that in an important sense it is God who ultimately brings it about that I experience the sensations that I do here, but nonetheless on Berkeley's account it is my mind's decision to direct its attention in various directions that indirectly causes me to experience the sensations that I do. (In the same kind of way, we might say, it is my mind's decision that I should press the buttons that I do on my computer games console controller that prompts the computer program to alter the things I can see on my computer screen as my character runs this way and that way under my control). In both of these cases, the mind is exercising its *will*, or its faculty of 'volition' as Berkeley sometimes calls it, and in doing so is demonstrating its ability to be an active thing.

I've explained earlier why Berkeley thought that we can't perceive any mind (including our own) by sense perception, and indeed that we can't in fact even have an idea of a mind (see above, p. 57).

Instead, he has it that I know of my own mind by direct or immediate 'intuition' or (to use an alternative term) by 'reflexion' (see, *e.g.*, *Principles* §89; *Dialogues* pp. 231–2). He doesn't say a great deal in fleshing out exactly what he means here, but the kind of thought he seems to be articulating is that it is just very obvious and transparent to me that I have a mind, and that I'm aware of its existence by some kind of 'inward feeling', as he puts it. Indeed this seems to be the same kind of account that Berkeley's predecessor René Descartes gave when he famously claimed that 'I think, therefore I am' (see above, p. 29). For Descartes too, the fact that I exist (that is, my mind exists) is a 'single intuition' or 'simple insight' that's immediately obvious to me and beyond doubt whenever I think or perceive.

Be that as it may, do you think Berkeley's got it right when he claims that it's very obvious and transparent to you that you've got a mind, and that you're aware of its existence by some kind of 'inward feeling'? Do you yourself experience anything that answers to the (admittedly vague) description of such a feeling? One person who thought that we experience no such thing was the eighteenth-century Scottish philosopher David Hume (1711–1776). He claimed that when we 'introspect' (or look inwards or inside ourselves, figuratively speaking), the only things we are aware of are the various thoughts, ideas and perceptual experiences that we have. There is no extra thing, a 'mind', to be found – no additional thing that we are aware of here over and above the thoughts, ideas and experiences themselves. Do you think that Hume's got a point? Or do you perhaps think that Berkeley's got it (at least kind of) right when he says that there is something that it feels like to have your mind, over and above the various thoughts and ideas that you have?

Quite how I can come to know that minds other than my own exist on Berkeley's account is a good question. After all, according to him minds aren't among the things I'm aware of when I perceive using my senses, and the inward feeling or direct intuition that I have when I'm aware of my own mind presumably doesn't tell me about the existence of any minds other than my own. We'll return to Berkeley's answer to this question later on in this chapter (see below, pp. 104–6), once I've said a good deal more about the role of God in his philosophy.

God's mind

The mind that is God ('the divine mind' or the 'infinite mind') runs the whole show in Berkeley's philosophical system. It's God who created our minds, and it's God who produces in our minds the ideas that make up the tables and chairs and all the rest of the contents of the world around us (see, *e.g.*, *Principles* §149; *Dialogues* p. 232). He does this in such a fantastically complex yet well-designed and seamless way that the objects we experience out there in the world around us all behave in regular, constant and law-governed ways, we each experience the right things at the right time, and we all experience the same things when it's appropriate that we should do so. To give two very simplistic examples, having produced in my mind the ideas that constitute my knee smacking against the edge of the table, as a result of my choosing to move my leg in a certain way, God then produces in my mind a feeling of excruciating pain. And when both you and I are looking in the same direction, God produces in each of our minds simultaneously the ideas that constitute, say, the pub that we both can see.

An incomplete analogy here would be that God is running a virtual reality computer program in which we all participate, a program which causes us each to have the sensations that we do – the arrays of colours, smells, 'feels', sounds and tastes that constitute the objects that exist around us in the virtual world. If you like, Berkeley's world of everyday objects is like the multi-person virtual world that the machines create for the human subjects to experience in the film *The Matrix*. The reason why this kind of analogy is incomplete is that of course, for Berkeley, there is no 'real world' beyond the virtual reality which we can come back to once we stop engaging with the computer program in question – the world we experience, which is the world God is running for us when he produces ideas in our minds, *is* the real world.

In order to be able to do all this, obviously God must be fantastically powerful and intelligent, and indeed Berkeley's God is the God of Christian orthodoxy, with the traditional divine attributes of omnipotence, omniscience, being all good and so on. Berkeley's God knows everything that we do, and indeed everything that can be known, and because He's intimately involved in the production in our minds of the ideas that constitute the world around us, He is constantly and intimately involved in our lives. We'll see later on in this chapter quite how Berkeley attempts to *prove* that God exists, and we'll encounter one or two philosophical problems that he potentially faces in placing God so centrally at the heart of his system. In the next instance though I want to say more about the role God plays in keeping the everyday objects around us in exist-ence, and I'm going to do so by introducing the two ways in which Berkeley maintains that everyday objects continue to exist even when there's none of us around to perceive them.

iv. HOW EVERYDAY OBJECTS CONTINUE TO EXIST WHEN THERE'S NONE OF US ABOUT TO PERCEIVE THEM

We are already well acquainted with the fact that Berkeley is an *immaterialist* (he maintains that there is no such things as matter or material objects), and also with his claim that everyday objects are collections of ideas. However, this by itself isn't quite enough to qualify him as an *idealist*. There are in fact *two* main forms that immaterialism can take – *idealism* and *phenomenalism*.

Idealism, in Berkeley's context, is the theory that everyday objects are collections of ideas, and that their *esse* is *percipi*. That is, the existence of the table, for example, consists in the fact that it is being perceived *right now*, and the ideas which constitute the table are *actual* ideas which are being had by someone *right now*. Meanwhile phenomenalism (again in Berkeley's context) is the theory that everyday objects are collections of ideas, and that their *esse* is **either** *percipi* **or** *posse percipi*. That is, the existence of the table, for example, consists in the fact that it is **either** being perceived *right now*, **or** it *would* be perceived, *were* we there to perceive it. The ideas which constitute the table this time are *either* actual ideas which are being had by someone right now, *and/or* potential or possible ideas which again we would have in various other circumstances.

Most of the time, Berkeley explicitly signs up to idealism. How-ever, as we will soon see, there are occasions when he at least appears to talk in phenomenalist terms. I want to illustrate the subtle but important difference between the two theories by addressing the following question: If everyday objects like tables and chairs are nothing other than collections of ideas, and specifically perceptual ideas, how can they continue to exist when no one's around to perceive them?

This is the kind of question we might well want Berkeley to give a satisfactory answer to. If it turned out, on his account, that tables and chairs didn't continue to exist when no one was around to perceive them – if, perhaps, they just popped into existence whenever we came into the room and disappeared again when we left – then we might be perfectly justified in rejecting Berkeley's philosophy as just plain daft.

As it happens, some Berkeley scholars maintain that he wasn't in fact all that interested in this question of 'object continuity', as we might call it. According to this view, Berkeley wasn't fussed whether or not his system allowed objects to continue to exist when no one was there to perceive them. I think that Berkeley was very much interested in this question though, and what's more, he was keen to show that objects *do* continue to exist after all, even when no one is in the room for example. For one thing, Berkeley took himself to be a champion of common-sense. He thought (regardless of what *we* might think) that it was his philosophy, and not the traditional, materialist philosophy, that allowed us to say, for instance, that we can indeed see and touch real objects, that we can know what these objects are like, and that they are just like we perceive them to be (see below, pp. 97–8). It would be strange to think that this self-proclaimed champion of common-sense wouldn't be bothered if his philosophy entailed that tables and chairs just popped into and out of existence as we entered and left the room.

Moreover though, Berkeley does answer the question of object continuity. Let's have a look at the two kinds of answer that he gives – the answer that he normally gives (his idealist answer) and the other answer that he sometimes gives (his phenomenalist answer).

Berkeley's idealist answer

Berkeley's better known and most usual answer is that everyday objects continue to exist when none of us is around to perceive them because *God* perceives them all the while. There's a famous limerick which alludes to this kind of answer, which you may have heard of. (The first verse is by the early twentieth-century clergyman and wit Ronald Knox; the second verse is most usually thought to be an anonymous reply):

> There once was a man who said 'God
> Must find it exceedingly odd
> If He finds that this tree
> Continues to be
> When there's no one about in the Quad.'

> 'Dear Sir: Your astonishment's odd:
> *I* am always about in the Quad
> And that's why the tree
> Will continue to be,
> Since observed by, Yours faithfully, God.'

We see Berkeley talking in these terms, although without explicitly using the word 'God', both in the *Principles* (*e.g.*, §§6 and 48) and in the *Dialogues* (*e.g.*, pp. 230–1). On this account, the *esse* of everyday objects in most definitely *percipi* – it is *actual* ideas that someone is having right now which constitute tables and chairs. In the case of the tables and chairs that none of *us* is perceiving at this present moment in time, it is the ideas of them in God's mind which keep them in existence.

The claim that the ideas which constitute everyday objects are *actual* ideas which are being had *right now* (by us and/or by God) is in tune with one of Berkeley's tenets that he is quite insistent on in various places. He tells us in no uncertain terms that an idea's very existence consists in its being actually perceived – for him, the notion of an idea that is not being had by someone right now just doesn't make sense (see, *e.g.*, *Principles* §6 and *Dialogues* p. 234). But

for example, He doesn't suffer pain, how can He know what pain is like? However, it is a particularly pressing problem for Berkeley, given the central roles played by sensations and God in his philosophy. It seems that either Berkeley must give up at least one of the claims that led to the *impasse* in the first place, or he must find a way of persuading us that his various claims aren't inconsistent after all. Have a think about it. Maybe I've been too quick in dismissing Philonous' response to Hylas here – for instance, is there any sense in which Berkeley could consistently claim that God can know *intellectually* what we know by sense perception. Or perhaps there's another way in which Berkeley could get round the problem. Then again, do you think that Berkeley's right when he says, for example, that someone can only come to an awareness of what a given sensation is like by having the sensation in question?

Whatever the case may be, it's this kind of problem that might lead us to ask whether it's possible to 'do Berkeley without God' – that is, whether it's possible to remove God from Berkeley's theory without completely destroying it. One way in which some Berkeley scholars have tried to 'do Berkeley without God' is by turning to the other, less well-known answer that he sometimes gives to the question of object continuity – an answer that sees him speaking in *phenomenalist*, rather than *idealist*, terms.

Berkeley's phenomenalist answer

On occasion, Berkeley says that everyday objects continue to exist when none of us is around to perceive them in the sense that we *would* perceive them *were* we around to do so. Here, he invokes what we *would* see in what philosophers call 'counterfactual' perceptual circumstances – the *fact* of the matter is that we happen to be in the study, but *counterfactually*, if we *were* in the billiards room we *would* see the dead body on the floor. In this way, the ideas that constitute the objects that continue to exist when none of us are there to perceive them aren't *God's* ideas, but the ideas we *would* have *were* we there.

We can see Berkeley talking in these kinds of terms in both the *Principles* and the *Dialogues*. At §3 of the *Principles*, he claims that the table he is writing on exists, 'that is, I see it and feel it', and that when he says it exists in the case that he's not in his study, he means 'that if I was in my study I might perceive it, *or* that some other spirit actually does perceive it' (my emphasis – here Berkeley is offering us alternately his phenomenalist answer and then his idealist answer). And later in the same work, at §58, he proposes that the question of whether the earth moves 'amounts in reality to no more' than the question of 'whether we have reason to conclude' from astronomers' observations that if we *were* placed at a certain distance from the earth we *would* perceive it moving with respect to the other planets. In the *Dialogues*, when Philonous remarks on p. 238 that although we don't perceive the earth's movement from our present location, it's wrong to conclude that we wouldn't perceive it were we placed a great distance from the earth. And Philonous explains later, on p. 251, that he imagines that if he had been present when God created the world, he would have seen things come into being in the order Moses describes in the Bible.

Now it may already have struck you that this kind of answer, given that it accounts for the continued existence of objects when we're not there in terms of ideas no one is actually having right now, is at odds with Berkeley's insistence elsewhere that ideas (and hence the objects they comprise) *can't* exist unless someone is actually perceiving them. This is just to say that Berkeley can't *consistently* uphold both claims, as he seems to want to. At least one of them has to go. Whether or not a case can be made for one or the other of them being less important for Berkeley's overall project is a complicated question that we won't go into here. Suffice to say, some people are led to view Berkeley's phenomenalist moments as a mistake on his part, or perhaps as something that he didn't really mean. Other people though, often those who want to try to 'do Berkeley without God', endeavour to make room for it.

This issue of consistency aside, what else might we ask in assessing the plausibility of this second kind of answer that Berkeley gives to the question of object continuity? One criticism that is sometimes made is that, on this account, the objects we aren't perceiving right now don't have the 'full-blooded' kind of existence that we typically want to say they have. Take an object that no one is presently perceiving – say one of the moons on the far side of Saturn. We normally think that this object exists in just as 'full-blooded' a sense as does the book that you're looking at now. But according to Berkeley's phenomenalism, *none* of the ideas which constitute that moon are being perceived right now. So doesn't that make the existence of that moon somewhat flimsy, or 'non-real'?

As it goes, Berkeley himself wouldn't necessarily have been too worried about this kind of criticism. In the third of the *Dialogues* there's a passage on pp. 251–2 where Hylas and Philonous are discussing how it might be said that God created various things *before* man came into existence, and hence before we were able to perceive them. Philonous is perfectly happy to concede such presently unperceived objects have a *real* existence, albeit one that is *hypothetical* or *relative*. That is they exist only on the *hypothesis* that *were* we there to perceive them, we *would*, and their existence is defined *in relation to* what we would perceive in those counterfactual circumstances.

Nonetheless, you can still ask whether this *hypothetical* or *relative* existence is enough for your philosophical tastes. Just ask yourself though – what are your philosophical tastes informed by here? As some Berkeley scholars note, if you'd only be satisfied by the claim that unperceived objects are to be credited with the kind of *mind-independent* existence that materialists maintain that they have, then you're not being particularly fair to Berkeley. You'd be assessing the plausibility of Berkeley's account of the nature the existence of unperceived objects by *materialist* standards. But given that Berkeley is an *immaterialist*, he can hardly be expected to live up to these materialist standards. To criticize him for failing to do so would be like complaining that his immaterialist account of the nature of the existence of unperceived objects turns out to be a bit, well, immaterialist. If you do want to criticize this specific part of Berkeley's philosophy, you'd be better off arguing that the existence of unperceived objects on his account isn't 'full-blooded' enough by something other than materialist standards.

Meanwhile, there's something of a debate among Berkeley scholars about whether it is even possible to think about 'doing Berkeley without God', for example by attributing to him a phenomenalistic method of accounting for the continued existence of objects in the absence of the likes of us that doesn't make any reference to God. According to some, it doesn't make any sense to suggest that we can 'do Berkeley without God', since combating atheism and affording God a central role in his philosophy in such a way that He can be seen to be directly and intimately involved in every step of our lives were concerns of the utmost importance to Berkeley. Scholars who take this view tend to treat his phenomenalistic moments as essentially 'theocentric' in character (that is, they unavoidably involve reference to God). For example, some people claim that at the heart of Berkeley's phenomenalistic account of object continuity are God's *volitions*. Here, the reason why we would have certain perceptual experiences were we in various counterfactual perceptual circumstances is that God has decided that we should.

But even if it is true that we simply can't take God out of Berkeley and claim that we're still dealing with Berkeley, we can nonetheless ask whether he *gives us the tools* to do immaterialism without God. Let's run for the moment with a phenomenalism which makes no reference to God. On this view, objects (which are collections of the perceptual ideas we presently have *and* the perceptual ideas we *would* have *were* we in various counterfactual perceptual circumstances) continue to exist when none of us is around in the sense that we *would* perceive them *were* we around to do so. Can immaterialists who don't want to involve God in their philosophy plausibly account for the continued existence of everyday objects in this way? One of the further questions we could ask such immaterialists under this head is the following. What explanation can we give for *why* we have the perceptual experiences that we do? For example, why is it that every single person in the library simultaneously has the visual, tactual and auditory sensations *etc.* which make up the library that they're all aware of? And why is it that we *would* have the sensations that make up a moon on the far side of Saturn *were* we in the right perceptual circumstances? Materialists are in a position to answer this question. According to them, the material objects themselves out there in the mind-independent world beyond us cause us to have the perceptual experiences that we do, for instance by reflecting lightwaves in such a way that they register on our retinas and ultimately bring about the visual experiences we have of the objects in question. So too, Berkeley is in a position to answer this question when he brings God into the equation. On his standard account, we have the perceptual experiences we do because God directly produces them in our minds. But without material objects and without God, what possible explanation could there be for why we have these perceptual experiences? It seems that a 'God-free' phenomenalism would present us with a massive and perhaps intolerable mystery here.

Should this be such a big problem though? This question of why we ultimately have the perceptual experiences that we do is perhaps simply akin to the other 'big' questions that people ask today, such as 'why are we here?', and 'why is there something in existence in the first place, rather than nothing?' Many of us think that we *can't* answer these kinds of question, and that it's no sleight on our philosophical worldview that we can't. *If* that's right, and *if* this analogy is a just one, (and these might be pretty big 'ifs') then perhaps it would be unfair of us to demand to know from a 'God-free' phenomenalist why we happen to have the perceptual experiences that we do. Perhaps the answer will be 'we just do', and that's all that can be said on the matter.

It's time to move on now from the question of object continuity. We'll be returning to the topic of God again later on, when we examine Berkeley's attempts to prove that He exists. For now though we're going to take a look at Berkeley's answers to some of the other questions that can be asked of his philosophy.

v. THE REALITY OF THINGS AND THE DISTINCTION BETWEEN REALITY AND ILLUSION

One popular criticism of Berkeley's philosophy, which he himself anticipated and responded to, is that he does away with the 'real world' – that, since everyday objects are collections of ideas and in this way are 'just in the head', there's no sense in which there's a real world out there anymore. And of course there is *a* sense in which 'the real world' no longer exists on Berkeley's account. If by 'real world' you mean 'mind-independent material world', then he is guilty as charged. But given that Berkeley is an immaterialist, to accuse him of doing away with the mind-independent material world is as trivial as it gets.

However, if by 'the real world' you mean the world of everyday objects that we see around us, the world of tables and chairs which feel hard to the touch, which different people can perceive, which continue to exist when we're not there, and which can be distinguished from the tables and chairs that I conjure up in my imagination or which the hallucinating madman claims to be aware of, then Berkeley cannot be fairly accused of doing away with the real world. On his account, we really do have the ideas that constitute everyday objects. These ideas are *real* – they comprise one of the two basic kinds of thing that there are in existence (see above, p. 56), and the collections of ideas which comprise everyday objects are similarly real. What's more, everyday objects as Berkeley understands them even pass a famous test of reality that was proposed by his predecessor John Locke – if you doubt that the fire in front of you is real, simply plunge your hands into it and you'll soon find out that you're mistaken (see Locke's *Essay* – Book 4, Chapter 11, Section 8).

Crucially, on Berkeley's account, reality exists despite the fact that there is no mind-independent material realm. What he has done is to change what it is that the word 'reality' refers to (see, *e.g.*, *Principles* §36; *Dialogues* p. 258). Instead of referring to mind-independent material things, Berkeley uses the term to refer to our ideas. But not just any old ideas – or else it would be the case that the unicorn I've just dreamt up exists in reality. Rather, he reserves the term 'reality' for the ideas that constitute the objective world around us.

Indeed, by reserving the word 'reality' for certain of our ideas, Berkeley thinks that it's his theory alone that allows us direct contact with reality and that allows us to know what reality is like (see, *e.g.*, *Principles* §§34–5; *Dialogues* pp. 211–12 and 229). His materialist predecessors claimed that the 'real world' was the mind-independent material world, but they also claimed that what we are aware of in the first instance when we perceive using our senses was something *other* than this mind-independent material world – namely ideas in our minds (see above, p. 44). Consequently the likes of Descartes, Malebranche and Locke are sometimes accused of cutting us of from reality – if all we're aware of in the first instance are our own ideas or mental experiences, how can we know what the mind-independent, material world is like beyond our ideas or experiences, or even whether there is a mind-independent material world in existence in the first place? As philosophers put it, Indirect Realists risk stranding us behind the 'Veil of Ideas' or the 'Veil of Perception', unable to get beyond our own ideas to find out anything about reality whatsoever. (Berkeley himself makes this precise point, though without using the term 'Veil of Ideas', for example at §18 of the *Principles* where he argues that if there were 'solid, figured, moveable substances' existing beyond the mind, we should know nothing of them, even on the materialists' account, because all we are aware of in the first instance when we perceive using our senses are our own ideas.)

Some people think that Berkeley's predecessors in fact *do* proceed to give us the means to beyond the 'Veil of Ideas' and in touch with reality. Be that as it may, by making reality consist in our ideas themselves, Berkeley takes himself to be ripping down the veil altogether – there is no gap, for him, between the ideas that we have when we perceive the world with our senses and reality itself, for the ideas and reality are one and the same thing. As a result, he thinks that it's his own theory, rather than the theory of his materialist predecessors, that's in tune with the demands of common-sense here – that there is a real world out there, and that we can perceive it and know what it is like.

Berkeley also flags up a further, related way in which he takes his philosophy to accommodate our common-sense intuitions about the way things are. Recall how philosophers in the seventeenth and eighteenth centuries typically maintained that, for instance, the colour we experience an object to be isn't really a genuine property of that object as it is in and of itself (see the section on the "distinction between Primary and Secondary Qualities' above, pp. 46–50). Rather, the colour we experience is essentially something to do with us and the reactions we happen to have to the way the object really is. So in an important sense here these three philosophers were claiming that everyday objects don't *really* have the colours we experience them to have – so that, for example, the apple isn't *really* green. And likewise for all of the other Secondary Qualities, at least as they were commonly defined. (Locke of course had a slightly different account – see above, pp. 49–50.) So a banana isn't *really* sweet, a drum-kit isn't *really* noisy and velvet isn't *really* soft to the touch. But this isn't how things seem to us (or at least not at first). To us, the apple does look as though it *really* is green – the greenness strikes us as being out there, *on* the apple. And the drum-kit does sound as though it *really* is noisy – and the sound it makes strikes as coming from over there, where the drum-kit is. That is, the claim that Secondary Qualities aren't real, genuine properties of objects as they are in and of themselves, independent of us, seems to fly in the face of the way we take the world to be on the basis of our perceptual experiences. Berkeley is keen to point out though that on his account, everyday objects really do have the properties we experience them to have (see, *e.g.*, *Dialogues* pp. 229–30). So, for example, the apple really is green, because the green sensations we have when we look at it are part of the collection of ideas that *is* the apple, and so on for each of the other examples. Again, he takes it to be the case that it is his philosophy, unlike that of his predecessors, that allows us to say in truth that we perceive everyday objects as they really are, and that we are in direct contact with reality (because we are in direct contact with the ideas that make it up).

One thing that Berkeley's materialist opponents did find easy was drawing a sharp distinction between reality and illusion. For them the real world is the mind-independent material world out there, whereas illusions are 'just in the head'. Given that Berkeley brings reality 'into the head' by identifying it with ideas, how can he distinguish between reality on the one hand and illusion on the other? Does his philosophy leave us any way of telling apart real things from figments of the imagination? If it doesn't, we'd be right to dismiss it as hokum.

In fact Berkeley draws the distinction between reality and illusion in various ways. On occasion he invokes the fact that we *can't help* but have the ideas that we do when we perceive the real world using our senses – having the ideas that constitute reality is not subject to our will (see, *e.g., Principles* §§ 29 and 33; *Dialogues* pp. 214 and 235). Of course we can choose whether or not to open our eyes, but if we do, we can't help but have the perceptual experiences that result. Whereas we can choose to summon up, alter and extinguish 'creatures of the imagination' at will (such as the idea of a unicorn that I'm presently contemplating). He sometimes puts the same point another way by noting that the ideas we have that constitute reality are caused to appear in our minds by God, whereas the ideas that constitute figments of our imagination are caused to appear in our minds by us (see, *e.g.*, Principles §33; *Dialogues* p. 235).

At other times, Berkeley points to the fact that the ideas that comprise real objects are, for instance, more vivid, striking, lively, constant and internally coherent than those that comprise figments of our imagination (see, *e.g., Principles* §§30, 33 and 36; *Dialogues* pp. 215 and 235). To give an example that illustrates the kind of thing he has in mind here, compare what you are aware of when you look at a real carrot with the mental image of a carrot that you summon up when your eyes are closed. The latter at best seems to be a pale, 'watered-down' version of the former, and the former is present to your consciousness in a much more striking fashion than the latter.

And in at least one place Berkeley also remarks that real objects are those that can be experienced by a number of people simultaneously (with the implication that only I can be aware of the figments of my own imagination) – see *Principles* §84.

However, even taken in conjunction with one another, these three features (which very often do allow us to distinguish reality from illusion) are not enough to *guarantee* that a given set of ideas is a real object rather than a figment of the imagination. This can easily be shown by appealing to the commonly-cited counterexample of a shared, systematic hallucination or illusion. Such hallucinations or illusions (though doubtless rare) may not be subject to the will of those experiencing them, may appear perfectly vivid, striking, lively and internally coherent, and may be experienced by a number of observers. This would be the case, the standard counterexample continues, when a number of people can all see what looks to be an oasis in the desert, when in fact there is no such thing in existence after all. So Berkeley needs to give us something more, another tool we can use to distinguish reality from vivid, internally coherent hallucinations or illusions that a number of people can't help but see. And in fact he does.

The telling distinction between real objects and the objects that feature in hallucinations and illusions on Berkeley's account is that the ideas that comprise real objects ultimately behave in the right kinds of way in relation to other actual and possible ideas (see, *e.g.*, *Principles* §§30 and 36; *Dialogues* p. 235), whereas the ideas that comprise even shared and systematic hallucinations and illusions do not. Even the most thorough-going hallucination will be at odds with other ideas we will have, even though at the time of the hallucination those experiencing it may not be in a position to tell that this so. For instance, in the case of the shared hallucination of an oasis in the desert, those experiencing it can soon find out that it was merely a mirage, when they 'walk towards it' and find that there is no water there after all. For Berkeley, the crucial distinction between real objects and hallucinations, illusions or other figments of the imagination consists in the fact that the former alone behave, in the fullness of time, in the right sorts of way in accordance with the Laws of Nature.

vi. DOING SCIENCE AND NAVIGATING OUR ENVIRONMENT

The point I've just made is important – real objects on Berkeley's account are *law-governed*, in the sense that God produces the ideas in our minds that make up real objects in regular, orderly ways. As a result, the real objects (*i.e.*, the sets of ideas) in question *behave themselves*. For example, whenever we measure the temperature at which water starts to boil (in normal conditions), the thermometer reads 100°C – and this happens despite the fact that there are no material objects in existence. In Berkeley's system, the reason why the thermometer always reads 100°C when the water starts to boil is that God, having brought about the ideas in our minds that constitute the water starting to boil, consequently brings about the ideas that constitute the sight of the thermometer reading 100°C.

Every time. Berkeley's world, just like what materialists take to be the real world, and just like a virtual world in a computer game, takes the form of a giant orderly network of causes and effects. Only in Berkeley's case it isn't a computer program or the blind laws of nature acting on material objects that's responsible for the causal network being as it is; it's God's direct, constant and law-governed production of the ideas in our minds.

And because the world of ideas is run by God in this regular and orderly fashion, we have everything we need to be able to navigate our environment (just as we might say that we are given everything we need by a computer game program to navigate the environment of the game). Indeed this is a point that Berkeley insists on (see, *e.g.*, *Principles* §§30–1; *Dialogues* p. 229). What we experience in our waking lives are ideas cropping up in various regular and ordered patterns, and it is the behaviour of these ideas in accordance with the patterns we have observed which allows us to go about our business. People today would typically admit that we are able to successfully navigate our environment because we see, feel, hear, taste and smell what we do, and because the things we experience here behave in regular, orderly ways; and the same is true on Berkeley's philosophy. He simply offers his own account of the *metaphysics* (*i.e.*, the fundamental nature of reality) that underpins our experiences. Crucially, we would experience what we do *regardless* of whether or not Berkeley has got the metaphysics right, and it's *because* we experience what we do that we are able to get about, on Berkeley's system or any other.

So too, Berkeley maintains that it is because we experience what we do, in observing the habitual connections that obtain among the ideas we have when we perceive using our senses, that we are able to do science, to discover the Laws of Nature, and to describe the world in terms of causes and effects. To give an example, when we say that fire causes the water to boil in the pan, we mean that the observation of fire being placed under a pan is typically followed (eventually) by the observation that the water is boiling. On Berkeley's account, we habitually observe this to be the case because God, having produced in our minds the ideas that constitute the fire being placed under a pan, typically proceeds to produce in our minds the ideas that constitute the boiling water. In such cases 'cause' is the name we give to the prior or 'antecedent' event, and 'effect' is the name we give to the consequent event.

Now *ultimately* for Berkeley, the genuine cause of the fact that the water has started to boil (*i.e.*, the fact that the ideas that constitute the boiling water have appeared in our minds) is God. According to Berkeley, strictly speaking God is the *only* cause of the existence, nature and behaviour of everyday objects. In the example above, strictly speaking the *fire* doesn't cause the water to boil. The fire and the water are both collections of ideas, and as we've seen, ideas for Berkeley are *passive* – they don't have any power to bring about changes in anything else at all (see above, p. 57). Nonetheless, we can happily use 'cause-talk' to describe the world, for example by saying that the fire *does* cause the water to boil, and that the fire *is* the cause of the water boiling. It's just that when we talk in these terms, we should remember that we're not doing *metaphysics* (*i.e.*, we're not attempting to describe the way the world *ultimately* is); we're doing science. By calling something a *cause* here, we aren't saying anything at all about the *ultimate* reason why things are the way they happen to be. Instead, for Berkeley, we're simply describing what we see in a way we find handy (see, *e.g.*, Principles §51). In saying that the fire causes the water to boil, we are making reference to the fact that in our past experience the observation of fire being placed under a pan of water is typically followed by the observation that the water is boiling.

Similarly, for Berkeley, the Laws of Nature aren't intimately bound up with the existence of the material universe and the governance of material objects – obviously not. Instead the Laws of Nature are to be defined in the first instance as the rules that God chooses to impose on His production of ideas in our minds (see, *e.g.*, Principles §§30 and 32; *Dialogues* pp. 231 and 253). If we decide to heat some water to a sufficient degree, the rule that God decides to follow is that at the right time He will produce the ideas in our minds that constitute the water boiling. And because God's rule-governed production of ideas manifests itself in the regular and orderly experiences we have of the world, we can also talk about the Laws of Nature in terms of the habitual connections that we continually observe to hold between the ideas that make up the objects in the world (see, *e.g.*, Principles §§59 and 62; *Dialogues* p. 243). It is these habitual connections that allow us to explain what goes on in the world. For instance, we can say that this pan of water began to boil because we know on the basis of past experience that as a general rule (or 'Law of Nature') water beings to boil when we heat it sufficiently. And it is also these habitual connections that allow us to make successful predictions about what will happen in the future, such as the prediction that the next pan of water we heat sufficiently will also begin to boil. Obviously, I've just given you rather crude and overtly simple examples here, but insofar as doing science involves us explaining things and making predictions on the basis of our past experiences, there's no reason on Berkeley's account why we couldn't keep doing the incredibly complex science that we do today. After all, we'd have the experiences that we do and we'd observe just what we observe whatever the metaphysics. Whether our experiences and observations are caused by mind-independent material objects or whether they are caused directly by God, we'd still see what we see and feel what we feel, wouldn't we?

So Berkeley thinks that we can still do the whole of science on his account, so long as we don't claim to be doing metaphysics in the process, for example by postulating the existence of matter in our scientific theories. Indeed, he takes it to be the case that once matter is disposed of, we can do our science all the more easily (see, *e.g.*, Principles §§50 and 107; *Dialogues* pp. 241–2 and 257). But doesn't at least some science purport to describe matter and its properties? For example, scientists today tell us that there's a whole load of 'antimatter' out there somewhere, whose essential nature is defined in terms of and in contrast with that of matter, and that it would be very bad news for us if sufficient quantities of matter and antimatter came into contact anywhere near our vicinity.

In fact, whether our science today *does* describe the kind of mind-independent material substance that Berkeley took exception to probably depends on what you mean by the term 'matter'. If by 'matter' today's scientists mean a mind-independent substance which has certain mind-independent properties and behaves in certain mind-independent ways, then Berkeley's philosophy is obviously at odds with (some of) our science. (However, even in this case, the possibility might yet remain that Berkeley has got it right and the scientists have got it wrong with respect to the existence of matter.)

But if it's *not* essential to today's science that what we call 'matter' is a mind-independent material substance, then it's less obvious that there is a problem for Berkeley's philosophy here. Perhaps all scientists need to mean by 'matter' is something other than 'a *mind-independent* substance that *really does* exist'. For example, perhaps it would be enough for us to be able to do all the science we want if by 'matter' we simply mean something we're merely going to *hypothetically assume* the existence of.

Personally, I've no idea which metaphysical entities today's scientists require the *actual* existence of in order for science to work. If you're interested in this question, your best bet would be to ask a philosopher of science. What I do know is that Berkeley himself *is* prepared to allow us to keep using the *word* 'matter' if we find it useful to do so, for example in doing our science. If we find it so hard to do without the word, then so long as we don't use it to mean a mind-independent substance that really exists, and we use it instead to refer to the stuff or the bodies that we are aware of when we perceive using our senses (*i.e.*, collections of ideas) then Berkeley ultimately has no complaint. (see, *e.g.*, *Dialogues* pp. 261–2. Nonetheless even here Philonous cautions Hylas against using the word 'matter', precisely because it's a word which many people do take to mean a mind-independent substance that really does exist.)

vii. HOW WE KNOW THAT OTHER MINDS EXIST (INCLUDING GOD'S)

We're now going to return to a question that I put aside earlier, namely how it is on Berkeley's account that I can know that there are any other minds other than my own. After all, he says that I can't have an *idea* of a mind. For one thing, minds aren't among the things I'm aware of when I perceive using my senses. Moreover though, recall how Berkeley says that passive ideas can't possibly capture the essence of active minds, and so there can't be an idea which represents or is 'of' a mind (see above, p. 57). And again the inward feeling or direct intuition that I have when I'm aware of my own mind presumably doesn't tell me about the existence of any minds other than my own (see above, p. 83–4).

Of course you might say to me that you have a mind, and that you know this because you have an immediate awareness of its existence. Yet, as Berkeley himself acknowledges (at §148 of the *Principles*), all *I'm* directly aware of when I receive this information are various sensations of my own, such as the visual sensations I have when I see you standing there opening and closing your mouth and the auditory sensations I have when I hear you saying to me that you have a mind. I've not been given any *direct* evidence here that there's such a thing in existence as your mind.

Many people think that Berkeley faces a big problem here, one which could well be fatal to his whole philosophy. Specifically, Berkeley is thought to face the threat of 'solipsism'. Solipsism is the theory that the only thing that exists (or at least the only thing that I can *know* to exist) is my own mind and its contents, and traditionally it's been a view that no philosopher wants to be credited with on the grounds that it is so unpalatable. So is there any way that Berkeley can avoid the charge that he is a solipsist – that his philosophy cuts me off from knowledge of the existence of any minds other than my own?

Berkeley says there is, and indeed his own argument for the existence of other minds is very similar to the one we ourselves might give (see, e.g., Principles §§140 and 145; *Dialogues* p. 233). I know that I have a mind, and I know that it is responsible for much of the movement and behaviour of my body, including my speech. For example, given the beliefs and the desires that I have, I make up my mind to move my body in purposeful ways. My body's movement, behaviour and speech betray the fact that there is an intelligent mind directing it. And what I see in the world around me are other bodies, just like mine, also moving and behaving and speaking in what appear to be purposeful ways. Might these bodies just be mindless automata? Well, possibly. But in just the same way that *my* body's movement, behaviour and speech betray the fact that there is an intelligent mind directing it, so too the movement, behaviour and speech of each of these other bodies betray the fact that there are intelligent minds directing them. So even if I can't know for certain that there are other minds out there, and that it's not just a world containing my mind and the ideas it has (solipsism), I know by *analogy* with my own case that it's highly likely that there are.

Putting Berkeley aside for a moment, do *you* know for certain that there are other minds out there, and that what you take to be other people aren't just mindless automata? If so, *how* do you know? If you think that you can know for certain (or at least with a high degree of probability) that there are other minds, is your thinking along the same lines as Berkeley's? Any which way, do you think that there's anything about Berkeley's philosophy that ultimately prevents *him* from being able to rely on this kind of answer?

As it happens Berkeley himself anticipates one reason why it might be claimed that *he* can't help himself to the belief or knowledge that there are other minds in existence after all. At one point in the *Dialogues* (p. 232), Hylas complains that Philonous is guilty of double-dealing. Philonous had just argued that we can't even *conceive* of the existence of mind-independent matter, urging that the *very idea* turns out to be an empty nonsense, and that people who claim that there is such a thing as matter *quite literally* have no idea what they are talking about. In short, matter can't possibly exist because we can't even form an idea of it. (We'll examine this argument in more detail in the next chapter). Hylas' precise complaint now is that while Philonous discards the existence of matter on the grounds that we can't even form an idea of it, he is perfectly happy to grant the existence of minds, even though he thinks we can't form the idea of a mind. To be consistent, Hylas claims, Philonous must either admit the existence of matter or deny the existence of minds.

Hylas' complaint isn't a just one, however. For one thing he has overlooked Berkeley's restrictive definition of the term 'idea'. On Berkeley's account, ideas are the things we are aware of in the first instance when we perceive using our senses, feel passions like anger or fear or conjure up images in our imaginations. But ideas aren't the only kind of item our minds can contemplate – we can also have *thoughts* or *notions* of various things that aren't derived from our perceptual experiences (see above, p. 57). So while strictly speaking we can't have an *idea* of a mind, we can have a thought or a notion of one. Moreover, and this is Philonous' precise response to Hylas' complaint, the problem with matter wasn't just that we literally have no idea of it, but that the very idea of it would be a *contradiction in terms*. The very thought of mind-independent matter is thus an impossibility. The proposed existence of matter is a contradiction, a nonsense, something that can't possibly be. The very thought or notion of a mind, meanwhile, *isn't* a contradiction in terms, or a nonsense, or an impossibility. So in fact there's no double-dealing afoot here after all.

Berkeley's arguments for the existence of God

So much for other people's minds. But what about the divine mind that is God? How does Berkeley think we can establish that God exists? In fact he gives us two main arguments for the existence of God over the course of the *Principles* and the *Dialogues* – the 'Continuity Argument' and the 'Passivity Argument' as they are often called today. I should remark that there's disagreement among Berkeley scholars concerning which of these arguments he genuinely signed up to. For example, some people think that he didn't subscribe to the Continuity Argument, because they think that he wasn't really that fussed about the question of whether or not everyday objects continue to exist when we're not around to perceive them (see above, p. 87). However, traditionally Berkeley has been credited with both arguments, and you'll certainly find evidence of (at least something approaching) each argument in the primary texts. It will do for our purposes to take it as read that there are two arguments, and we can usefully study and think about each of them in turn.

The Continuity Argument

You'll find Berkeley's Continuity Argument for the existence of God on pp. 230–1 of the *Dialogues* (though see also *Principles* §6 and *Dialogues* p. 212). The starting point for the argument is the fact that everyday objects like tables and chairs continue to exist even when I'm not around to perceive them (that is, even when I'm not around to perceive, have, or be aware of the ideas that make them up). But given that the very existence of everyday objects consists in the fact that they are being perceived (their *esse* is *percipi*), then there must be some other mind that perceives them when I don't, in order for them to continue to exist. And the same is true for all other finite minds – there must be some other mind that perceives everyday objects, for example, when *you* don't perceive them. Indeed, the fact of the matter is that tables and chairs would continue to exist even if there were *no* finite minds around to perceive the ideas that constitute them. In this case there would still have to be *some mind or other* perceiving them in order to ensure their continued existence. So in the absence of all finite minds, there must be a mind that isn't a finite mind in existence that perceives the tables and chairs in question. That's just to say that there must be an *in*finite mind in existence, or to put the same thing another way, God must exist.

Are you immediately persuaded by this argument to accept the existence of God? Assuming that you aren't, your challenge is to be nice and precise in saying why not. What *exactly* do you think is wrong with this argument? If you can't pinpoint anything that's wrong with it then you're rationally obliged to accept Berkeley's conclusion, aren't you?

One thing that we can say about it is that the argument is clearly premised on (that is, it takes as its starting claim) the truth of Berkeley's idealism. It's only if everyday objects are collections of ideas whose existence consists in being perceived that there's any need to appeal to another mind perceiving them in my absence, or indeed in the absence of all finite perceivers. On the materialist philosophy, the continued existence of everyday objects in the absence of finite perceivers doesn't require the existence of some other mind to perceive them – material objects can continue to exist in the absence of *all* perceivers because material objects, unlike collections of ideas, don't need to be perceived in order to exist. So it's trivially the case that the success of Berkeley's Continuity

Argument for the existence of God depends for its success on his idealism being true.

But how's about we grant Berkeley his '*esse* is *percipi*' principle for everyday objects, for sake of argument. What else might we say about the Continuity Argument? One common criticism is that it's no good as an argument for the existence of God since it involves Berkeley arguing in a circle. According to this objection, Berkeley argues that we know that God exists because we know that everyday objects continue to exist in the absence of finite perceivers. But elsewhere hasn't he also claimed that we know that everyday objects continue to exist in the absence of finite perceivers, because we know that God exists and perceives them all the while? (See above, pp. 87–8.) In which case, Berkeley seems to be telling us that we know that God exists because we know that everyday objects continue to exist; and we know that everyday objects continue to exist because we know that God exists; and we know that God exists because we know that everyday objects continue to exist; and we know that . . . *ad infinitum*. On this view, Berkeley is just going round and round in circles. This kind of circular reasoning is typically rejected by philosophers as flawed, because someone who isn't *already* convinced either that God exists or that objects continue to exist in the absence of finite perceivers won't be persuaded by Berkeley's reasoning here to accept any part of what he says (see above, p. 22).

Does he argue in a circle though? It's clearly the case that he does *if* what he's saying is this:

> We know that objects continue to exist in the absence of finite perceivers; therefore we know that God exists. AND we know that God exists; therefore we know that objects continue to exist in the absence of finite perceivers.

The problem here is that the very thing that our knowledge of object continuity is used to prove (namely, our knowledge of God) is used in turn to establish that we have knowledge of object continuity in the first place. In other words, we're appealing to our knowledge of God to establish the thing that's required to prove that we have knowledge of God.

Yet *is* this what Berkeley says? Perhaps his claim isn't that 'we know that God exists; therefore we know that objects continue to exist in the absence of finite perceivers', but that 'it's God's existence which grounds the fact that objects continue to exist in the absence of finite perceivers'. The first claim is an *epistemological* one (to do with what we know and how we know it), whereas the second claim is an *ontological one* (to do with what exists). And it's not immediately obvious that Berkeley is arguing in a circle in just the same way if what he's saying is this:

We know that objects continue to exist in the absence of finite perceivers; therefore we know that God exists. AND it's God's existence which grounds the fact that objects continue to exist in the absence of finite perceivers.

Here, the thing that our knowledge of object continuity is used to prove (again, our *knowledge* of God) isn't the same as the thing we use to ground the fact of object continuity (namely, the *fact* of God's existence). So we're not appealing to our *knowledge* of God to establish the thing that's required to prove that we have knowledge of God. Rather we're appealing to the *fact* of God's existence to ground the thing that's required to prove that we have knowledge of God. Of course, it still remains open for someone to ask 'but how do you *know* that God's existence is a fact?' But Berkeley's answer to this question needn't make any mention of object continuity. For instance, he might appeal to his second argument for the existence of God, the Passivity Argument.

Whether or not Berkeley does ultimately argue in a circle in the manner I'd originally suggested he might is something I'll leave for you to think about. What do you see when you read what he actually says in the *Principles* and the *Dialogues*? Do you see something akin to the first and obviously circular line of reasoning above? Or perhaps you see something akin to the second line of reasoning that I've claimed isn't obviously circular in the same kind of way? This is just one example of a debate that you should aim to settle by consulting what a philosopher actually says in the primary texts (see above, pp. 15–16).

Another tack might be this. Perhaps Berkeley simply takes it as a given – an assumption that it's perfectly reasonable to make, and which doesn't need to be justified by an argument – that every-day objects continue to exist in the absence of finite perceivers. In this case, he wouldn't actually be *arguing* that 'God exists; therefore objects continue to exist in the absence of finite perceivers' (or even that 'we *know* that God exists; therefore we *know* that objects con-tinue to exist in the absence of finite perceivers'), and so he wouldn't be *arguing* in a circle after all. The question then would be, *is* Berkeley entitled to take it as a given that everyday objects continue to exist in the absence of finite perceivers. We ourselves take it to be completely obvious that they do – it's one of our beliefs that we don't typically feel any need to justify by way of *argument*. In which case, why can't Berkeley say the same thing? Is there any difference between our general philosophical outlook and Berkeley's that makes object continuity a perfectly reasonable assumption to make in our case, but not in his own?

One reason for thinking that there is such a difference revolves around Berkeley's insistence, which people today typically don't share, that an everyday object's *esse* is *percipi* – its existence consists in the fact that it is being perceived. It's this insistence which perhaps means that it's down to him to explain how it is that everyday objects continue to exist in the absence of finite perceivers. Meanwhile, *we* typically think that everyday objects are material objects whose *esse* is not *percipi*. We take it to be of the very nature of material objects that they do continue to exist in the absence of finite per-ceivers, and that consequently there's no need for us to go on to explain how they do.

Even so, we still can ask *why* we think that everyday objects are *material* objects. Can that view be justified, or is it perhaps just an assumption on our part that we hold for no good reason? If it's the latter, and we don't have a problem with this fact, would it be fair of us to criticize Berkeley for taking it for granted that everyday objects continue to exist in the absence of finite perceivers, should it turn out that this is what he's doing?

The Passivity Argument

Berkeley's Passivity Argument for the existence of God appears, for example, at §§29–30 and 146 of the *Principles* and on pp. 214–15 of the *Dialogues*. It starts with the premise that we can't help but have the experiences we do when we perceive the world using our senses. The perceptual ideas or sensations we get when we open our eyes, for example, come to us unbidden – *we* don't bring them about by *deciding* or *willing* that we should experience the sensations that we do. So, where do our sensations (our ideas of sense) come from? What brings them about? Berkeley, like many of his predecessors, accepts the doctrine that there can be no *creatio ex nihilo*, or 'creation out of nothing', so he rules out the possibility that our sensations just pop into existence out of thin air – no, *something* or *someone* must have caused them.

He maintains that it can't be *matter* that causally interacts with our senses and causes our perceptual experiences. Apart from the fact that he takes the existence of matter to be an impossibility, Berkeley notes that according to the materialist philosophers themselves, matter is supposed to be *inert* (see, *e.g.*, Principles §67–9; *Dialogues* pp. 257–8). That is, matter and material objects just sit there, waiting to be pushed around, acted on or otherwise changed. In and of themselves, they have no power to *originate* change, or to start a causal process that might end up with the production of ideas of sense in our minds. So too, Berkeley denies that our ideas of sense might be caused or brought into existence by other ideas. Recall that for him, ideas are entirely passive – they don't have the power to act on or bring about change in anything else (see above, p. 57).

Berkeley's conclusion is that whatever produces our sensations must be a *mind*, because according to him minds are the only active beings (or 'agents') in existence, the only things that can originate change and genuinely cause anything else to come to be. But what kind of a mind could have caused the sensations that we each experience? He's already ruled out the possibility that our own minds might have produced our ideas of sense – the fact that we can't help but have the sensations that we do when we perceive using our senses shows that their production isn't under our own control. So that would seem to leave us with two further candidates – either some other finite mind causes the perceptual sensations that we experience, or an infinite mind does. Which is it to be?

Our perceptual ideas themselves give us a clue here. The perceptual experiences that we each have are co-ordinated so neatly, are ordered in such regular, law-like patterns, and are so coherent with one another that they make up an entire *world*. What's more, this is a world not just that I am aware of, but that we're all aware of. And these facts testify to the vast power, wisdom and skill of the mind that produced them. There's only one mind that has sufficient power, wisdom and skill to bring about the entire, inter-subjective world of ideas that is the sum of our collective perceptual sensations; namely God. In short, because we have the perceptual ideas that we do, we know that God must exist.

What Berkeley has given us here is a combination of what philosophers call a 'cosmological' argument for the existence of God, and an 'argument from design'. (Cosmological arguments for the existence of God proceed from the question 'what caused this, that or the other?' and conclude that God did. Whereas arguments from design claim that the construction of this, that or the other indicates the prior presence of a designer, namely God).

As an aside, Berkeley also remarks that every bit of evidence that leads us to believe that there are other finite minds in existence is furthermore, and to a greater extent, evidence for the existence of God (see, *e.g.*, Principles §147). Recall how he thinks I can know that finite minds other than my own exist. I see that there are bodies very much like my own out there, behaving in the same kind of intelligence-betraying ways as mine does. I know that this intelligence-betraying behaviour in my own case is accounted for by the presence of an intelligent finite mind (my own) that's controlling my body's behaviour. So I've good reason to conclude that the intelligence-betraying behaviour of these other bodies out there is also to be accounted for by the presence of other intelligent finite minds just like my own. But moreover, Berkeley goes on to remark, the prior fact that there *are* ideas combining in such regular, orderly and coherent ways that they constitute these bodies in the first place is evidence that there must be a supremely intelligent and powerful mind in existence who produces them.

To return to the Passivity Argument itself, what do you make of it? For one thing, it's fairly obvious that the success of the argument this time depends on Berkeley being right when he tells us that what we are aware of when we perceive using our senses are *perceptual ideas* or *sensations* (rather than, say, material objects). If it's not the case that it's perceptual ideas that we're aware of here, then there can be no question of us invoking God to explain their occurrence. But suppose again that we temporarily grant for the sake of argument that all we are aware of when we perceive using our senses are ideas in our minds. We can still evaluate on *that* basis whether or not the Passivity Argument is any good.

Do you agree with Berkeley, for instance, that there can be no *creatio ex nihilo*, or creation out of nothing? His claim is that things (including our perceptual ideas) can't just pop into existence 'out of thin air', and we can ask whether he's right about this. Can you think of any counterexamples of things that do just pop into existence 'out of thin air'? Or is it perhaps implausible to think that things (including the ideas we have when we perceive using our senses) might just come into existence *for no reason whatsoever*?

In fact, it's sometimes proposed that Berkeley contradicts what he says in other places when he states that we ourselves couldn't create the perceptual ideas that we have, and more generally that there can be no creation out of nothing. He speaks at other times as if we do have the power to produce ideas 'out of thin air', namely when we conjure up ideas in our imaginations, such as the idea of a unicorn. In this case, we simply will the idea of a unicorn to be present in our minds, and – pffff – there it is. Now obviously there's a sense in which this kind of idea *doesn't* just pop into existence. We produce the idea of a unicorn by combining ideas that we've previously received from our senses (namely, the idea of a horse and the idea of a horn). Nevertheless, in between the time when we receive these component ideas from our senses and the time when we subsequently recall them and use them to create the composite idea of a unicorn, isn't it the case that we don't perceive them? If so, since he insists that the very existence of an idea consists in its being perceived, surely Berkeley is committed to maintaining that the component ideas don't exist in the interim. In which case, perhaps there is still an important sense in which we do create the idea of a unicorn out of nothing.

Even if we can create 'ideas of the imagination' out of nothing though, this claim isn't at all relevant to the present case. What Berkeley needs for the Passivity Argument is the more specific claim that our *perceptual* ideas can't just pop into existence 'out of thin air' – something or someone must have caused them, and we know for sure that it wasn't us. This brings us back round to a line of thought I touched on earlier in another context. *Must* there be an answer to the question of why we have the perceptual ideas or experiences that we do? (see above, pp. 94–5). My suggestion back then was that perhaps the only response we can give to this question is that 'we just do', and that's all that can be said on the matter. Whether or not this response strikes you as a miserable cop-out I'll leave for you to decide.

In this chapter, we've seen some of the central features of Berkeley's 'positive' philosophy – his own account of the way things ultimately are. He's told us that all we're aware of in the first instance when we perceive using our senses are ideas, and specifically sensations, and that everyday objects and their properties are nothing other than (collections of) these sensations. He's told us that ideas and minds are the only things that exist, and that it's God who creates and sustains the world around us by producing in our minds the perceptual experiences that we each have. Finally, he's told us how it is on his account that everyday objects continue to exist in our absence, how we can distinguish reality from illusion, how we can do science and navigate our environment, and how I can know that there minds other than my own (including God's). What we've yet to see are the various arguments and other strategies that Berkeley presents in his attempt to *prove* that immaterialism and idealism are true, and that's the business of the next chapter.

CHAPTER 4

BERKELEY'S ARGUMENTS FOR IMMATERIALISM AND IDEALISM

It's time now to take a look at the main arguments and other strategies that Berkeley uses in his attempt to *prove* that there can be no such thing as matter (his immaterialism) and that everyday objects are collections of ideas whose *esse* is *percipi* (his idealism). In the years since his death, many of Berkeley's arguments have been given names like the 'Argument from Conceptual Inseparability' and the 'Identity Argument' and so forth. Do be aware though that Berkeley didn't use these names himself, and indeed that different Berkeley scholars sometimes use different names for one and the same argument. I've adopted names that are commonly used, but even if you come across authors using alternative names it should still be fairly obvious which arguments they are talking about.

We'll begin by taking a look at Berkeley's starting claim that the things we perceive using our senses (including everyday objects and their properties) are (collections of) ideas, before examining what is known as his Master Argument. Many people take this argument to be little more than a crude piece of wordplay by means of which Berkeley perhaps tries to trick us into agreeing that mind-independent material objects can't exist by definition. I'll be aiming to persuade you that the Master Argument (at least as it appears in the *Principles*) isn't a crude piece of wordplay, but neither is it a *distinct* argument for the mind-dependence of everyday objects; rather it's a reiteration of a previous argument that follows on directly from Berkeley's starting claim that everyday objects and their properties are (collections of) ideas.

Next up we'll study a pair of arguments which Berkeley uses to try to defend his claim that various *properties* that we experience everyday objects to have are nothing other than ideas in our minds – the Argument from Perceptual Relativity and the Identity Argument. The Argument from Perceptual Relativity trades on the thought that the properties we experience everyday objects to have depend on the perceptual circumstances in which we find ourselves, and so these properties are essentially features of our own perceptual reactions to objects, rather than being genuine features of the objects as they are in and of themselves out there independent of perceivers. The Identity Argument meanwhile sees Berkeley claiming that (at least some of) the properties we experience objects to have are in fact identical with sensations of pleasure and pain, and hence can't possibly exist beyond the minds of those who are experiencing them.

Finally, we'll work through Berkeley's attack on abstract ideas and the arguments he bases on it. Here, for instance, we'll see him building on his *interim* conclusion that the properties we experience objects to have are nothing other than sensations in our minds by arguing that we can't even entertain the idea that there might be such a thing as matter in existence. For him, the very concept of matter is a meaningless nonsense.

Along the way, I'll present some of the common objections that have been raised by people who aren't convinced by his arguments. As I've mentioned previously, I think that all too often readers of Berkeley don't pay enough attention to his key claim that what we are aware of when we perceive using our senses are not just ideas, but are specifically *sensations*, and I'll put it to you that once we bear this key claim and his account of the nature of sensations in mind, some of these common objections to his arguments can be overcome. However, this method of defending Berkeley turns out to be something of a Trojan Horse, because the very claim on which the success of his arguments can be seen to depend is one he ultimately doesn't give us any good reasons to accept. Consequently, I maintain that Berkeley doesn't manage to *prove* immaterialism and idealism. Essentially he's arguing that immaterialism and idealism follow from the starting claim that what we perceive using our senses are sensations, but he doesn't do enough to establish that this starting claim is true.

Do be aware that in adopting the general strategy that I've just outlined, I'm presenting a rather *controversial* assessment of Berkeley's arguments, which is just to say that it's an assessment that many other people would disagree with. I think that it's the right assessment to make though, and that there are good reasons for drawing the conclusions that I do. I'll be presenting you with those reasons as we progress, and I hope that I'm able to persuade you to agree with me. However, you should bear in mind what I said in Chapter 1 about deciding for yourself whether or not you think Berkeley's arguments are any good (see above, p. 18). What I say with regard to the success or otherwise of Berkeley's philosophy is there as food-for-thought for you. Do you agree with me when I say the things that I do in evaluating his philosophical moves? If you think that I've got it wrong, that's fine by me – your challenge then is to say *why* you think I've got it wrong. If you think I've got it right, have a read of some other authors writing on Berkeley – you'll soon find someone who disagrees with what I say. Does what they write make you want to change your mind, or can you point to where you think *they* have gone wrong? In short, the most important thing for you to do in assessing whether or not Berkeley's arguments are any good is for you to work out what *you* think of them. If I can help you do that, I'll be very pleased.

i. BERKELEY'S STARTING CLAIM THAT THE THINGS WE PERCEIVE ARE SENSATIONS

Berkeley devotes the first eight sections of Part I of the *Principles*, and the first substantial exchange between Hylas and Philonous in the *Dialogues*, to an analysis of what it is that we're aware of when we perceive using our senses, and what we're referring to when we use terms like 'the things we perceive by sense', 'sensible qualities' and 'sensible things'. He makes it quite clear that what he's referring to when he uses these terms, and indeed what he thinks we're aware of when we perceive using our senses, are nothing other than sensations. On this basis, he immediately jumps to the conclusion that everyday objects too are nothing other than collections of sensations (given the obvious implication that everyday objects are among the things we perceive using our senses), and as such cannot exist beyond the mind. This early analysis of what it is that we're aware of when we perceive using our senses is crucial to Berkeley's entire philosophical project, so much so that it's worth working through each of the *Principles* and the *Dialogues* versions in turn in some detail, before we consider what might be said in a preliminary evaluation of what he's up to here. (You'll probably find it quite boring if you read these next two sections through by themselves. This is because they are designed to be a comprehension aid for the relevant passages in the primary texts. You'll hopefully find it less boring if you have a copy of the *Principles* and the *Dialogues* to hand, so that you can compare and apply my comments to what you see when you read Berkeley's original words).

Principles §§1–8

At §1, Berkeley counts 'ideas actually imprinted on the senses' among the 'objects of human knowledge' (*i.e.*, the things we can know about), and he then immediately proceeds to list the kinds of ideas we are given by each of our senses. His list includes a number of properties of everyday objects that many philosophers in the seventeenth and eighteenth centuries considered to be merely sensations in us (colours, the property of being hard or soft, odours, tastes and sounds – see above, p. 47), as well as a few items that would have typically been denied that status (light, motion, resistance). Berkeley then starkly asserts that everyday objects are collections of these ideas.

§2 mainly concerns the nature of the mind and its relation to ideas, and needn't delay us here. At §3, meanwhile Berkeley claims that it's obvious that everyday objects, being composed of 'sensations or ideas imprinted on the sense', can't exist beyond the mind. As I explained in Chapter 3, he uses the word 'or' in places like this to indicate that the different terms in question (in this instance 'sensations' and 'ideas imprinted on the sense') are alternative names for one and the same thing (see above, p. 58–9). This being the case, we can see here that Berkeley takes 'ideas imprinted on the sense' to be sensations, and indeed that he intends his §1 list of the various ideas that we're given by each of our senses to be a list of sensations.

Berkeley then continues later on in §3 to offer a justification for his claim that the objects which are composed of sensations can't exist beyond the mind. He explains what is meant when we say that 'sensible things' exist (and it's clearly implied here that he takes 'sensible things' to be another alternative term for 'sensations or ideas imprinted on the sense'). For example, he tells us that for an odour to exist means nothing other than it was smelled – or to put the same thing another way, an odour exists only so long as someone is having the sensation of the smell in question. This analysis, Berkeley claims, gives us 'intuitive knowledge' of the fact that objects which are composed of sensations can't exist beyond the mind. He also extends this analysis to other things he takes to be sensations, and the objects and properties he claims they comprise: sounds, colours, figures (*i.e.*, shapes) and tables exist only so long as someone is having the relevant sensation(s). To deny this, he claims, is 'perfectly unintelligible', and so his conclusion is that the existence of these things consists in the fact that they are being perceived – their *esse* is *percipi*.

In §4, Berkeley consolidates the analysis he's given us by reiterating that for 'sensible objects' (*i.e.*, collections of sensations) such as houses, mountains and rivers to exist when they are not being perceived would be a 'manifest contradiction'. Because these everyday objects are among 'the things we perceive by sense', they are 'our own ideas or sensations', and (as he proposed in §3) it is 'plainly repugnant' that sensations or combinations of sensations should exist beyond the mind.

Moving on to §5, Berkeley repeats the claim that (combinations of) sensations can only exist insofar as they are being perceived by someone (that is, insofar as someone is having the relevant sensations), and he immediately proceeds to list what he takes to be 'the things we see and feel', this time including extension (the property of being spread out in two or three dimensions) and figures (*i.e.*, shapes). He then states that these things too are nothing but 'sensations, notions, ideas or impressions on the sense' – another instance of Berkeley using these alternative terms synonymously. He goes on to tell us that to even try to think that 'sensible things' (*i.e.*, sensations) might exist without someone perceiving them (*i.e.*, without someone having the sensations in question) is to try to commit an unacceptable act of 'abstraction'.

By this he means that we're trying to abstract or *sieve out* from the initial idea of a 'sensible thing' a further idea that we can't possibly entertain. In this case, we're trying to sieve out from our idea of some sensations that are perceived by someone the idea of some sensations that aren't perceived by anyone – the latter idea of course doesn't even make sense. He then claims that to try to think of a 'sensible thing' (*i.e.*, a sensation or a collection of sensations) that exists but that no one is perceiving is like trying to 'divide a thing from itself' – it's something that cannot be done. And finally here, Berkeley attempts to reinforce his claim (that we can't even think of a 'sensible thing' that no one is perceiving) by introducing a maxim that will be central to his attack on abstract ideas – that we can only conceive separately (*i.e.*, think of separately) those things that can either exist separately from one another in reality or that we can perceive separately from one another using our senses (see below, pp. 163 & 179–80).

Section 6 sees Berkeley stating that it's very obvious that everyday objects can't exist beyond the mind, and that again it is 'perfectly unintelligible' and an attempted act of unacceptable abstraction to suggest otherwise. He then backs up this statement with a challenge: just *try* to conceptually separate (*i.e.*, separate in your thoughts) 'the being of a sensible thing from its being perceived'. The obvious implication here of course is that you can't. And indeed we can see that this challenge makes complete sense if we bear in mind that in talking about 'sensible things' Berkeley is talking about sensations. Because 'sensible things' are sensations or collections of sensations, to try to think of a 'sensible thing' that exists but that no one is perceiving is to try to think of a sensation or a collection of sensations that presently exists but that no one is having or that no one is aware of – an impossibility.

At §7, Berkeley argues that it follows from his thesis (that the existence of 'sensible things' consists in the fact that they are being perceived) that there can be no unthinking substance (*i.e.*, matter) in existence, only thinking substances (*i.e.*, minds). This he takes to follow without the need for any further proof, but he offers such proof anyway, by claiming that the 'sensible qualities' (*i.e.*, the properties we experience everyday objects to have when we perceive using our senses) are 'ideas perceived by sense' (*i.e.*, sensations), and he lists some of the usual suspects as examples – colour, figure, motion, smell and taste, in this instance. He claims now that it is a 'manifest contradiction' for an idea (and in this case, a sensation) to 'exist in' (that is, to be a feature of or to be present in) anything that does not perceive. In short, Berkeley is claiming that when it comes to the basic substances which underlie the 'sensible qualities', there can't be an 'unthinking substance' (*i.e.*, matter), because the 'sensible qualities' are ideas and an unthinking substance can't have ideas. There can only be 'thinking substances' (*i.e.*, minds), because only minds can have ideas.

Finally at §8, Berkeley anticipates an objection to what he's said so far that derives from the Representative Realist's account of what we are aware of when we perceive the qualities or properties of 'body' (*i.e.*, of everyday objects). Namely, that even though our perceptual ideas themselves (obviously) don't exist beyond the mind, the qualities or properties that they copy or resemble (or that they are ideas 'of') do (see above, p. 45). In reply, Berkeley produces his mantra that 'nothing can be like an idea but an idea', and more specifically that 'a colour or figure can be like nothing but another colour or figure'.

Again this reply makes clear sense given that what he specifically means by 'idea' here is 'sensation', and given that he takes colour and figure to be examples of sensations. As I claimed in Chapter 3, Berkeley maintains that there can be nothing like a sensation in existence beyond the mind, and that (for example) there can be nothing like a sensation of colour other than another sensation of colour (see above, p. 64). What he's essentially doing in §8 is arguing that there can't be anything out there in the mind-independent material world that resembles our perceptual ideas, because our perceptual ideas are sensations in our minds and the only thing that can resemble (*i.e.*, be like) sensations in our minds are other sensations in our minds.

His last move in §8 is then to complete his reply to the objection that the things our ideas copy or resemble (or are 'of') might exist beyond the mind by presenting a dilemma (*i.e.*, a choice between equally unpalatable alternatives) to those who might raise this objection. **Either** the proposed mind-independent originals that our ideas copy are perceivable, in which case they are themselves ideas, and specifically sensations (since the things we are aware of when we perceive using our senses are nothing other than sensations). **Or** the proposed mind-independent originals are not perceivable, in which case they can't resemble our ideas and so can't be represented by them, because nothing can be like an idea but an idea.

In summary, in §§1–8 of the *Principles*, Berkeley starkly *asserts* that the things we're aware of when we perceive using our senses are nothing other than sensations, and on this basis he draws the conclusion that everyday objects are nothing other than (collections of) sensations (given the assumption, which he heavily implies, that everyday objects are among the things we're aware of when we perceive using our senses). If Berkeley offers us any justification for his initial assertion that what we're aware of in perception are sensations however, this amounts to no more than the suggestion that it is obviously true. His next move is to flesh out the fact that sensations can only exist so long as they are perceived (*i.e.*, so long as someone is having them), and to apply this fact to 'sensible qualities', 'the things we perceive by sense', and everyday objects (on the basis of his earlier claim that these are all nothing other than sensations or collections of sensations). In other words, Berkeley directly concludes on the basis of his claim that everyday objects are collections of sensations that everyday objects cannot exist beyond the mind. And in claiming that 'nothing can be like an idea but an idea', he is again invoking (what he takes to be) an uncontroversial feature of the nature of sensations to rule out the possibility that the ideas we have when we perceive using our senses resemble and in doing so represent to us material objects and their properties existing out there beyond the mind.

Dialogues pp. 174–5 and 183

Pretty much right at the start of the *Dialogues* (as soon as the introductory niceties, Hylas' profession of astonishment at Philonous' immaterialism, and their agreement on the definition of scepticism are out of the way), Philonous sets out the same sort of stall as we've just seen in *Principles* §§1–8. He defines 'sensible things' as 'those things which are perceived by the senses'; only this time he's even more careful in his definitions than he was in *Principles* §§1–8 – he restricts 'the things perceived by the senses' to those things that are 'perceived immediately'. What Philonous intends by restricting 'the things we perceive by the senses' in this way is that we should rule out from the things we're aware of in sense perception anything we have to *infer* from what our senses tell us: anything that we have to infer in this way is by that fact alone not something that we *perceive*. Philonous then proceeds to list the things we immediately perceive by each of our senses, and it's pretty much the same as the list of sensations given in §§1–8 of the *Principles*: lights, colours, figures, sounds, odours, tastes, and 'tangible qualities' (*i.e.*, properties of objects that we perceive via the sense of touch). If this list is intended to be a list of sensations (as I think it is), then Philonous has claimed that 'sensible things' (*i.e.*, the things we are aware of when we perceive using our senses) are nothing other than sensations.

What Philonous certainly does claim subsequently is that 'sensible things' are nothing other than (collections of) 'sensible qualities' (the properties that we experience everyday objects to have when we perceive using our senses), which means (on my reading) that 'sensible qualities' too are sensations. He then moves on immediately to attempt to prove that each and every one of the 'sensible qualities' cannot exist beyond the mind. Unlike Berkeley in *Principles* §§1–8, Philonous doesn't state explicitly at this point that everyday objects are collections of the sensations we have via our senses. Nonetheless, the implication is clear. On p. 173 Hylas as good as accuses Philonous of 'denying the real existence of sensible things', a charge that Philonous rejects. It is obvious that Hylas, in making his accusation, intends 'sensible things' to be those everyday objects that sceptics deny we can have any knowledge of – a definition which Philonous accepts in denying the charge. If this is right, Philonous implicitly counts everyday objects among the 'sensible things' which he claims are nothing other than sensations.

Moreover, Philonous does extend his early analysis of key terms like 'sensible things' and 'sensible qualities' to everyday objects on p. 183, concluding there that these too are nothing other than sensations. Here, Hylas has just claimed that there are objects beyond the mind that really do have that colours that we see on them. Philonous reminds Hylas that they had agreed that the only things we perceive using our senses are the things we perceive immediately, and that the only things we perceive immediately are 'sensible qualities' (*i.e.*, sensations). He then has Hylas clarify that he takes a 'corporeal substance' (the proposed object that exists beyond the mind) to be something other than a collection of 'sensible qualities' (*i.e.*, sensations), before offering Hylas a dilemma: either 'corporeal substances' are 'sensible qualities' (*i.e.*, sensations), or they are not. If it's the latter, then we are aware of something other than 'sensible qualities' when we perceive using our senses. Since the second option here is contrary to their previously agreed definitions, Philonous concludes that the 'corporeal substance' (*i.e.*, the proposed object that exists beyond the mind) is in fact nothing other than 'sensible qualities' (*i.e.*, sensations).

Preliminary critical evaluation of Berkeley's early analysis

In a nutshell, so far Berkeley has starkly asserted (without yet offering us any reasons to think that he's right) that the only things we're aware of when we perceive using our senses are (collections of) sensations. From this starting point, and on the heavily implied assumption that 'sensible qualities' and everyday objects are among the things we perceive, he quickly concludes that 'sensible qualities' and everyday objects themselves are (collections of) sensations.

One thing that we can note straight away is that here Berkeley has presented us with a *valid* argument (see above, p. 21). The premises of the argument (that the only things we're aware of when we perceive using our senses are sensations, and that 'sensible qualities' and everyday objects are among the things that we perceive), if true, would by themselves guarantee 100% that the conclusion is also true – that 'sensible qualities' and everyday objects themselves are (collections of) sensations. The question is, is it a *sound* argument (see above, p. 22)? *Are* the premises true? If they're not, the argument is no good, despite the fact that it's valid.

Presumably, we can take it that the second premise – that 'sensible qualities' and everyday objects are among the things that we perceive – is obviously true, so I'm not going to worry about that claim here. But what about the first premise – that the only things we're aware of when we perceive using our senses are sensations? It's this claim that's at the very heart of Berkeley's philosophy, and on which his whole system in fact depends. So, is it *true* that all we're aware of when we perceive use our senses are sensations? Most people take it to be the case that we are aware of many things other than sensations when we open our eyes or feel around us with our hands *etc.* – not least, everyday material objects like tables and chairs. And it's perhaps for this reason that Berkeley is even more careful with his early definitions in the *Dialogues* than he was in the *Principles*. As we've seen, Philonous states that by 'the things we perceive by sense', he means the things we *immediately* perceive by sense – that is, the things we're aware of *in the first instance* when we perceive using our senses, before our minds jump to consider either anything else that these things suggest to us, or anything that we *infer* from them. In which case, Berkeley's starting claim is this: all we are aware of *in the first instance* when we perceive using our senses are sensations. So is *this* claim true?

There are various things that we might say in assessing this claim, but I want to focus on just one to get you thinking here. Take visual perception as an example. As I explained in Chapter 3, Berkeley maintains that what we are aware of in the first instance when we open our eyes is just an array of patches of colour, some of which have more sharply defined edges than others, and some of which move around in our visual fields as we turn our heads *etc.* (see above, pp. 59–60). My suggestion back then was that Berkeley's claim that all we are really given in the first instance in visual perception are colours is akin to the claim all we are given in the first instance when we look at a colour television screen is an array of coloured pixels, or that all we are given in the first instance when we look at a painting is an array of coloured dabs of paint. Does it strike you that there's a sense in which all you're really aware of in the first place when you open your eyes is an array of colours in this way? If you can, and if you're happy enough to grant that what we're experiencing when we perceive colour is a *sensation* of a certain kind (and these are perhaps both pretty big 'ifs'), then I think that you're well on your way to agreeing with Berkeley's starting position.

And you can ask the same question for the perceptual experiences we have via touch, hearing, smell and taste. When you run your hands over an object, do you recognize a sense in which all you're really aware of in the first place is an array of 'feels'? And when you hear something, do you think that there's a sense in which all you're really aware of in the first place is an array of sounds? When you're aware of the smell of coffee or the taste of pineapple, would you agree that there's a sense in which all you're really aware of in the first place is a particular sensation or experience that's 'as close to you as your own ideas', as Berkeley might say? Again if so, and you're satisfied that the 'feels', sounds, smells and tastes that you experience here are themselves perceptual *sensations* of various kinds, you might well be tempted to agree with Berkeley's initial claim.

Some people report that they can easily recognize a sense in which all they are really aware of in the first place when they perceive with their senses are arrays of sensations in this way. Other people report that they can't. As for myself, on occasion I've found myself having a 'Berkeley moment' when I'm walking down the street or some such, when it just strikes me as incredibly obvious that all I'm really given by my senses first up are sensations. At other times, the very suggestion strikes me as ludicrous, and I take it to be plain that what I'm immediately aware of are material objects out there in the world beyond me.

One person who agreed that it is just very obvious that what we're aware of when we perceive using our senses are material objects out there in the world beyond our minds was Dr. Samuel Johnson, the famous dictionary-writing man of letters (1709–1784 – not to be confused with Rev. Dr. Samuel Johnson, an American clergyman and philosopher who was a good friend and correspondent of Berkeley's). In a famous incident reported by his biographer James Boswell, Johnson responded to Boswell's suggestion that Berkeley's arguments for immaterialism and idealism are impossible to refute by booting a nearby stone and proclaiming 'I refute it thus'. Johnson was clearly of the view that the testimony of our senses themselves reveal beyond doubt that it is material objects out there beyond our minds that we encounter in perception.

As it happens though, Johnson's response to Berkeley here has the reputation of being one of the weakest objections to any philosophical theory that has ever been made, and this is because it completely misses the point. Suppose that Berkeley was right in claiming that there are no material objects in existence and that God directly creates the perceptual ideas in each of our minds. What would Johnson have experienced when he kicked the stone then? Precisely what he experienced when he kicked the stone. So, Johnson failed to appreciate that he couldn't appeal to his perceptual experiences themselves to demonstrate that those perceptual experiences weren't directly produced in his mind by God in the absence of material objects.

Nonetheless, it *is* controversial to claim that what we're aware of when we perceive using our senses are ideas or experiences in our own minds. There are theories of perception that have been articulated by philosophers in Berkeley's day and since, according to which we are *directly* aware of objects out there in the material world when we perceive using our senses. According to Direct Realism, for example, it's not ideas that we are aware of when we perceive using our senses, just objects out there in the material world (see above, p. 45). What's more, it's also controversial to claim that we aren't aware of (features of) mind-independent material objects when we experience the sensations that we do. There are contemporary theories of perception held by some philosophers today which state that our sensations do record features of mind-independent material objects. 'Externalist' versions of a theory of perception known as 'Intentionalism' maintain that this is the case, for instance. Whether these alternative accounts of perception are themselves any good is another question, though we needn't go into any of the details here. It's enough for our purposes for me to flag up to you that it's an ongoing matter of debate whether it's ideas that we're aware of (at least in the first instance) when we perceive using our senses, and whether sensations can reveal to us (either directly or indirectly) features of a mind-independent material world. Consequently, there's more for you to think about, if you're of a mind to, in deciding whether or not you're convinced that Berkeley's right in claiming that all we're aware of when we perceive using our senses are sensations, and that these sensations can't represent a material world to us because 'nothing can be like a sensation but a sensation'.

II. THE MASTER ARGUMENT

In the *Principles* (§§22–4), and again in the *Dialogues* (pp. 200–1), Berkeley presents what has become one of the most notorious arguments in the history of philosophy – his so-called Master Argument. According to the standard interpretation, here Berkeley claims that we can't even think of an everyday object that no one is thinking of, because in trying to do so *we* are thinking of it ourselves. So everyday objects can't exist 'unthought of' – that is, they can't exist beyond the mind. Most people who read Berkeley take this argument to be nothing more than a cheap attempt to use wordplay to trick us into agreeing that everyday objects are mind-dependent. It's worth working through and commenting on both the *Principles* version and the *Dialogues* version, so that you can decide what *you* make of it.

The *Principles* version

§22 of the *Principles* sees Berkeley claiming that the non-existence of matter can be proven very simply, by the very attempt to conceive that it's possible for the supposed properties of everyday objects to exist beyond the mind. He then asserts that the very concept or thought of properties of everyday objects existing beyond the mind is a contradiction (*i.e.*, a nonsense), and Berkeley is so confident of this that he offers his readers a challenge. If they can conceive that it is even possible for 'one extended moveable substance' (*i.e.*, any object) to exist beyond the mind, he will concede the existence of mind-independent matter.

Berkeley then moves on in §23 to present and reply to what he foresees as a potential response to his challenge, namely the claim that we can imagine trees existing when there is no one there to perceive them. His reply is that this doesn't count as an adequate response to his challenge. Here, we'd have simply entertained an idea whose content features trees, but doesn't feature any perceivers stood there looking at the trees. Yet it fails as an example of conceiving that it is possible that 'the objects of your thought' (*i.e.*, the things your thoughts are about) exist beyond the mind. Indeed it's a 'manifest repugnancy' that they should, for when we try to think of 'bodies' existing beyond the mind, we are in fact only 'contemplating our own ideas'. It's a delusion to think that we can and do think of bodies existing beyond the mind – these bodies are 'apprehended by or exist in' the mind.

Finally, at §24, Berkeley concludes that the concept of the 'absolute existence of sensible objects' beyond the mind is either contradictory or meaningless.

The *Dialogues* version

Philonous presents the Master Argument in response to Hylas' suggestion that while individual properties of objects cannot exist beyond the mind, combinations of them ('sensible things') might yet. Here, Philonous lays down the familiar challenge to Hylas – if he can even conceive of the possibility of any combination of properties (any 'sensible thing') existing beyond the mind, Philonous will concede the issue. Hylas tries to answer this challenge by claiming that he can conceive that (for example) a tree can exist beyond all minds, and he claims to entertain this very thought there and then. Hylas admits subsequently that it's contradictory to claim that you see something that at the same moment exists unseen, and that it's just as contradictory to claim that you can conceive something that is unconceived. He finally admits that his candidate reply to the challenge fails since it amounts to nothing more than framing an idea whose content features a tree, but doesn't feature a perceiver stood there looking at the tree, and that he hasn't conceived of everyday objects existing beyond all minds after all.

Two common objections to the Master Argument

Again it's often thought that the Master Argument is either woefully naïve or, more likely, a crude piece of underhand chicanery, and that it turns on the trivial truth that the *thought* that you have when you think of something, being a mental item, resides in the mind. Now, it is certain that the argument involves the claim that everyday objects can't exist unconceived (*i.e.*, beyond the mind) because the very concept of them doing so involves a contradiction. And it's commonly taken to be the case that the contradiction in question is supposed to derive from the simple fact that in any attempt to conceive of an object existing unconceived, you conceive of the object yourself, which renders the attempt unsuccessful.

Given this interpretation of the argument, people typically think that the Master Argument can be easily defeated. Yet some commentators do think that there is more to the Master Argument than first meets the eye, and there's a tendency here to think that it should be interpreted in the light of the arguments Berkeley gives us elsewhere against the possibility of abstract ideas. (We'll encounter Berkeley's attack on abstract ideas in due course – see below, pp. 161f.) The claim here is that the Master Argument can be seen to be a better argument than is commonly supposed once we take his arguments against abstract ideas on board. Those who want to interpret the argument in this way though may well face a problem, as some of the commentators in question themselves admit. This is because Berkeley seems to insist in both the *Principles* and the *Dialogues* that the Master Argument *taken by itself* is enough to secure the downfall of materialism. I'll have more to say about how I think the Master Argument should be interpreted in a short while. Before then, let's take a look at two common objections to the argument as it's usually interpreted.

A first common objection (presented for instance by Jonathan Dancy in his book *Berkeley: An Introduction*) is that even if it were a valid argument (*i.e.*, even if the premises, on the assumption that they are true, would by themselves guarantee 100% that the conclusion is also true), the Master Argument as it stands is irrelevant to the fate of materialism. This is because the argument could only establish the wrong conclusion as far as Berkeley is concerned. Far from establishing that there can be no such things as objects existing beyond the mind, the Master Argument would only show that the objects that we're thinking of *right now* do not exist unthought of *right now*. However, the materialist's claim is that everyday objects *could* exist unthought of *at some time or other*, and it's no contradiction, for example, to think of a tree that will be unthought of tomorrow.

Another common objection is that, as it happens, the Master Argument *isn't* valid, because it could only go through if we run together (or 'conflate') two distinct meanings of the term 'unconceived' that should in fact be kept separate. When we consider a given conception we can think about it insofar as it is a thought in our heads, in which case it's very obvious to say that conceptions can only exist in the mind. Here indeed we can't conceive of the unconceived by definition, both in the sense that we can't have a thought that's not being thought about, and in the sense that we can't have a thought that exists beyond the mind (because all thoughts reside in the mind). But we can also think about a given conception in terms of whatever it is that the conception is about, or is a conception 'of'. And it seems perfectly possible to conceive *of* something that exists unconceived (*i.e.*, that exists beyond the mind), even if while you're thinking of it, it's not unconceived (*i.e.*, not being thought of). According to the present objection, what Berkeley does in the Master Argument is to slide between these two meanings of the term 'unconceived', and in doing so he makes a big mistake (and quite possibly a deliberate one in an attempt to bamboozle us). If we keep these two meanings separate, we'll see that the Master Argument fails. Or so the objection goes.

A reinterpretation of the Master Argument

I'll come back to these two objections in a bit. First though, I want to explain how *I* think the Master Argument should be interpreted. Under this head, let's consider Berkeley's apparent insistence that the Master Argument is enough on its own to spell the end for materialism. In §22 of the *Principles* version, Berkeley worries that he has already gone to unnecessary lengths in 'handling this subject' (*i.e.*, arguing that there's no such thing as matter – that this is the subject he has in mind is made clear in §21), since the case can be proven with certainty and to anyone's satisfaction in a couple of lines. He then declares that he is 'content to put the whole' (*i.e.*, rest his entire case) on the single issue of whether or not one can even conceive of objects existing beyond the mind, before immediately proceeding to present the Master Argument. Likewise, in the *Dialogues* version Philonous states that he too is 'content to put the whole' on the same issue, and he also states that he is prepared to 'pass by all that hath been hitherto said, and reckon it for nothing'. At a first glance then, this all suggests that Berkeley thinks that the Master Argument in isolation is enough to defeat materialism.

However, I think that we need to be a little more careful in deciding what (for instance) Philonous means when he says that we can 'pass by all that hath been hitherto said'. Taking the *Principles* version first, we should note that Berkeley spends §§1–8 setting up his *definitions* of terms like 'sensible qualities', 'sensible objects' and 'the things we perceive by sense' and outlining his starting *premises* that the things we perceive by sense are nothing other than sensations, and hence that everyday objects are collections of sensations. He then devotes §§9–21 to presenting a range of arguments against the existence of matter, many of which ultimately depend on the initial definitions and premises which he established in §§1–8 (as we'll see later in this chapter). I suggest that it's natural to understand Berkeley to be referring to the range of arguments in §§9–21 when he worries that he has gone to unnecessary lengths in arguing against the existence of matter. He seems to me to be telling us that the Master Argument will suffice in place of any of the *arguments* that he'd recently introduced. This however doesn't mean that he intends his readers to also overlook the initial definitions and premises that he carefully presented at some length in §§1–8.

So too in the *Dialogues* version, recall that the Master Argument is presented in response to Hylas' objection that although individual properties of everyday objects don't exist beyond the mind, the 'sensible things' that they comprise might yet do so. Philonous then reminds Hylas that the two of them have already gone through the 'sensible qualities' one by one to show that they don't exist beyond the mind, and summarizes the Argument from Conceptual Inseparability that Philonous had presented earlier. (We'll examine this argument later in this chapter – see below, pp. 163 5). Philonous then remarks that 'this was not the only argument made use of on that occasion', and the text at the top of p. 200 makes it clear that the other arguments he's referring to by implication here are ones that he'd previously introduced to prove that figure (*i.e.,* shape) and motion could not exist beyond the mind. As we'll soon see, these other arguments (such as the Argument from Perceptual Relativity – see below, pp. 150f.) again depend on the starting claim that the things we perceive using our senses (including everyday objects) are nothing other than sensations, which as we've seen was agreed on at pp. 174–5 of the *Dialogues.* So when Philonous comes to present a new *argument*, in the form of the Master Argument, for the conclusion that 'sensible objects' do not exist beyond the mind, I suggest that there's no reason to suppose that Philonous intends Hylas to abandon the initial definitions and the starting premise they had agreed on at the beginning of their discussion. I think that what Philonous has in mind when he says that he's prepared to 'pass by all that hath been hitherto said, and reckon it for nothing' is that the Master Argument will suffice in place of any of the previous *arguments* that have been covered (the Argument from Perceptual Relativity, the Argument from Conceptual Inseparability *etc.*), but not in isolation from the definitions and premises that were agreed on at the start.

In summary, I maintain that it's *not* the case that Berkeley bans us from considering the Master Argument in isolation from *anything* he's said previously when he announces, for example, that we can 'pass by all that hath been hitherto said'. It's reasonable to take him to be saying that the Master Argument will do instead of any of the other *arguments* that he'd recently introduced against the existence of matter. But I don't think that it's reasonable to take him to be saying in the same breath that we can also ignore his understanding and definition of key terms such as 'sensible quality', 'sensible object' and 'things perceived by sense'. Indeed, it doesn't really make sense to suggest that Berkeley would think that the Master Argument could be presented against a backdrop of key terms that were *anyhow* defined. All philosophical arguments should proceed from agreed definitions and premises, and Berkeley spends some time at the start of both the *Principles* and the *Dialogues* presenting us with his. My conclusion is that the Master Argument should be interpreted in the light of his early definitions of the terms 'sensible quality', 'sensible object' and 'the things we perceive by sense', and his starting premise that the things we perceive by sense, including everyday objects, are (collections of) sensations.

And if we now take on board Berkeley's starting premise that the things we perceive by sense, including everyday objects, are (collections of) sensations, a different interpretation of the Master Argument emerges, and it's worth working through both versions once more to see the extent to which this is the case.

The *Principles* version revisited

At §22, as we've already seen, before he challenges his readers to try to conceive of an object existing beyond the mind and before he presents the Master Argument, Berkeley states that the very concept of an object's properties existing beyond the mind is contradictory. Bearing in mind now his early definition of 'sensible qualities' as sensations, this would clearly be the case, since sensations are ideas and as such can't possibly exist beyond the mind. He then challenges his readers to try to conceive that it's even *possible* for 'one extended, moveable substance' (*i.e.*, any object) to exist beyond the mind. And of course, given that he takes everyday objects to be nothing other than collections of sensations (or more generally, ideas), it's *not* conceivably possible that objects defined as such can exist beyond the mind either.

Now at §23, in considering the proposal that we might imagine trees existing when no one's there to perceive them, Berkeley concedes that it is possible to entertain an idea whose content features trees, but doesn't feature any people stood there looking at the trees. But he denies that this counts as an example of conceiving that it's possible that the things one's ideas are ideas *of* might exist beyond the mind. He notes that it's a 'manifest repugnancy' that they should do so. And again, given his starting premise that everyday objects are collections of sensations (or more generally, ideas), it *is* repugnant (*i.e.*, contradictory) to claim that they might exist beyond the mind. On his account it is quite literally the case that when we try to conceive 'bodies' existing beyond the mind we are in fact only 'contemplating our own ideas' (and specifically, sensations), because 'bodies' are nothing other than collections of sensations. Indeed, it's a delusion to think that we can and do conceive of 'bodies' (*i.e.*, collections of sensations) existing beyond the mind. As collections of sensations, these 'bodies' must be 'apprehended by' and can only 'exist in' the mind.

And once more, given his starting premise that everyday objects are nothing other than collections of sensations, it's wholly reasonable that Berkeley concludes at §24 that the very concept of the 'absolute existence of sensible objects' beyond the mind is either contradictory or meaningless.

If my interpretation is right, we're now in a position to see that the standard reading of the *Principles* version of the Master Argument identifies *the wrong contradiction*, and in doing so misstates the nature of Berkeley's claim when he says that we cannot conceive the unconceived. The contradiction that the Master Argument trades on *doesn't* derive from the fact that any supposedly unconceived object you're thinking of is in fact conceived of by you. Rather, it's the contradiction that's involved in the supposition that a collection of sensations can exist beyond the mind.

Furthermore, the standard interpretation of the Master Argument can now be seen to 'put the cart before the horse'. It's *not* in fact the case that the impossibility that an everyday object might exist beyond the mind *follows* from our failure to conceive of a given object that does exist beyond the mind. On my interpretation, our inability to conceive of a given object that exists beyond the mind *follows from* the fact that ideas (and specifically, sensations) cannot exist beyond the mind. In challenging us to try to conceive that it's even possible that an everyday object should exist beyond the mind, Berkeley is trialling his earlier starting premise that the things we perceive, including everyday objects, are collections of sensations. And it's a challenge that he knows cannot be met given that sensations, as a species of idea, cannot possibly exist beyond the mind.

On my interpretation however, the *Principles* version of the Master Argument ceases to be a *distinct* argument for the conclusion that everyday objects cannot exist beyond the mind. Rather, it's merely a reiteration of the step in §4 where the same claim falls out directly from his starting premise that the things we perceive using our senses, including everyday objects, are (collections of) sensations. In which case, why does Berkeley bother presenting the Master Argument at all, if he's essentially just repeating what he'd already said some eighteen sections earlier? Well, that's a good question. One suggestion that I have is that Berkeley presents the Master Argument at §§22–4 to *remind* his readers that *even though* the arguments against the existence of mind-independent objects and their properties which he presented at §§9–21 are (in his view) successful, we shouldn't *forget* that the conclusion in question can be derived directly from the initial definitions that he presents in §§1–8. Another suggestion might be that Berkeley's purpose in presenting the Master Argument is to anticipate and respond to what he foresees as being the most natural objection to the claim that it's inconceivable that objects should exist beyond the mind, namely that it's a trivially simple task to imagine (and thus conceive of) them doing so. Note though that each of these suggestions would entail that the title 'Master Argument' for the argument we're given at §§22–4 in the *Principles* is something of a misnomer, insofar as it implies that Berkeley is presenting an altogether new argument, when in fact what he's doing is presenting afresh a step that we've already seen in condensed form at §4.

The *Dialogues* version revisited

In the *Dialogues* version however, it's far more tenuous to claim that Philonous is presenting the Master Argument as I've just reinterpreted it. Gone are the claims from the *Principles* version that can be interpreted as bold statements of the essential mind-dependence of objects, given Berkeley's early starting premise that everyday objects are collections of sensations. Instead, Philonous merely relies on the claim that any candidate conception of an unconceived object will be conceived by the person entertaining the concept, and thus the object itself is in fact conceived the whole while. That is, the standard interpretation of the Master Argument seems to be the one that's vindicated by the text of the *Dialogues* version.

What then are we to make of the fact that the *Principles* version is open to reinterpretation along the lines that I've suggested, whereas the *Dialogues* version isn't? Of course it could be claimed that this simply shows that my proposed reinterpretation of the *Principles* version of the Master Argument is just a red herring, and that in the *Principles* Berkeley never intended anything other than the standard interpretation of the argument after all. Perhaps it's simply a coincidence that his expression of the argument in the *Principles* is open to another interpretation.

My own view here is that Berkeley may well have intended two different arguments here – that, if you like, there are *two* Master Arguments. The *Principles* version proceeds along the lines that I've suggested in my reinterpretation above, whereas the *Dialogues* version in fact sees Philonous seizing on *another* way in which he thinks the things our ideas are ideas *of* can shown to exist in the mind and nowhere else. Rather than challenging us in the *Dialogues* version to conceive of a collection of sensations that can exist beyond the mind, he's challenging us to conceive of something that we're not conceiving of right now, just like the standard interpretation says he is.

Suppose that I'm wrong here though, and that my attempted reinterpretation of the *Principles* version of the Master Argument *is* just a red herring which Berkeley *didn't* actually intend to present –

what then? Well, it would still be the case that there is *a* version of the argument that Berkeley *could* have given had he wanted to, a version which does seem to be faithful to the text of the *Principles*, and which does apparently seem to make sense in the light of the starting definitions and premises that he lays down at §§1–8 of the *Principles* and on pp. 174–5 of the *Dialogues*. And if this reinterpreted version can evade some of the standard objections to the Master Argument, then perhaps it would have been a *better* argument for Berkeley to have presented. In which case, let's see how my interpretation of the Master Argument fairs in the face of the two common objections that I introduced earlier.

Two common objections to the Master Argument revisited

I take it to be plain that the two objections in question succeed in blowing the Master Argument as it's usually interpreted out of the water. How's about the *Principles* version of the Master Argument as I've interpreted it though?

The first objection was that even if the Master Argument succeeds in establishing that the things we're thinking of *right now* can't exist unthought of *right now*, this doesn't mean that material objects can't exist beyond the mind. It's still the case that material objects *could* exist unthought of *at some time or other*, and so it's not a contradiction to say, for example, that you're thinking of a tree that no one will be thinking of tomorrow. On my interpretation of the *Principles* version of the Master Argument however, Berkeley's claim is that it *is* a contradiction to say that everyday objects could exist beyond the mind *at any time*. This isn't because in conceiving of an everyday object that exists unconceived tomorrow you're conceiving of it yourself the whole while, but because everyday objects are collections of sensations, and sensations (or more generally, ideas) can't exist beyond the mind at *any* time. So it is in fact a contradiction to say that you're thinking of a tree that no one's thinking of tomorrow, because all trees, past, present and future, are collections of ideas whose *esse* is *percipi* – that is, whose very existence consists in the fact that they are being attended to by some mind or other.

Second up was the objection that even if the Master Argument at first seems to succeed, this is only because Berkeley is illegitimately sliding between two distinct meanings of the term 'unconceived'. While it is the case that we cannot conceive of something that exists unconceived in the sense that it's not being thought of by anyone right now, it's perfectly possible to conceive of something that exists unconceived in the sense that it exists beyond the mind. But again, on my interpretation of the *Principles* version of the Master Argument, Berkeley's claim is that it's in fact impossible to conceive of an everyday object that exists beyond the mind. After all, it follows from the early definitions and premises from which my interpretation of the Master Argument proceeds that everyday objects are collections of sensations; and of course we can't possibly conceive of sensations (or more generally, ideas) that exist beyond the mind.

In short then, my claim is that if we pay close attention to the Master Argument, we'll see that (at least the *Principles* version) isn't a distinct argument for the non-existence of matter that can be taken in isolation from everything else Berkeley has said. Rather, it should be interpreted in the light of his early definitions of terms like 'sensible quality', 'sensible object' and 'things perceived by sense', and his starting premise that the things we perceive using our senses, including everyday objects, are (collections of) sensations. Interpreted in this way, the *Principles* version doesn't trade on the claim that we can't conceive that it's even possible for an everyday object to exist unconceived in the sense that we're not presently conceiving of it, but on the claim that sensations (or more generally, ideas) can't possibly exist beyond the mind. And interpreting the Master Argument in this way allows us to reject some of the common objections that are levelled at it. Whether or not you agree with me here, and whether or not the Master Argument on *any* interpretation can avoid some of the other objections that you'll find elsewhere if you read around, I'll leave for you to think about.

iii. THE IDENTITY ARGUMENT

Berkeley uses the Identity Argument in an attempt to prove that some (if not all) of the properties that we experience everyday objects to have are indeed nothing other than sensations, and as such cannot possibly exist beyond the mind. And in trying to prove that at least some of the properties we experience everyday objects to have are sensations, Berkeley is aiming to give us a good reason why we should accept that at least some of things we are aware of when we perceive using our senses are in fact sensations. (Recall that he had *asserted* early on in both the *Principles* and the *Dialogues* that *all* of the things we are aware of when we perceive using our senses are (collections of) sensations. At the time he didn't offer his readers any reasons *why* they should think that this is the case. What we have with the Identity Argument is the beginning of Berkeley's attempt to make good on that starting claim.)

The Identity Argument appears in its fullest form on pp. 175–8 in the *Dialogues*, with an extension on pp. 179–81 and a possible rejoinder on pp. 191–2. Here, Philonous tries to demonstrate that a number of an object's properties *as we experience them* cannot exist beyond the mind.

(An aside is in order at this point, by way of introduction. Many philosophers think that there is a distinction to be drawn between an object's properties *as we experience them* and those same properties *as they are in the object*. Take the property of being hot as an example. It's often claimed that heat *as we experience it* is to be characterized in terms of the particular experience you have when you feel that an object is hot, whereas heat *as it is in the object* is to be characterized in terms of the activity of the surface molecules of the object – the faster the molecules are moving, the hotter the object is. Now obviously there's a correlation between heat *as it is in the object* and heat *as we experience it*. Typically, the faster the surface molecules of an object are moving, the hotter we experience it to be. But crucially, according to this distinction, what we're directly aware of when we experience an object to be hot *isn't* the surface molecules of the object moving about (*i.e.*, we're not directly aware of the heat *as it is in the object*) – rather, what we're directly aware of is an experience or a feeling of a certain character, a feeling which those who've had it know fine well, but which can't be adequately described in terms of the movement of molecules on the surface of the object. What Berkeley is trying to do with the

Identity Argument is to establish that the experiences or feelings that we have when we perceive certain properties of objects using our senses are in fact sensations.)

The properties of objects that Berkeley explicitly considers when he presents the Identity Argument are the properties of heat and cold, and, later on, tastes and odours. His general strategy is to claim that these properties *as we experience them* are in fact identical with (*i.e.*, one and the same thing as) entities that obviously can't exist beyond a perceiving mind, namely sensations of pleasure and pain.

Philonous and Hylas start off by considering the property of heat. The Identity Argument's first premise here is that either all degrees of heat exist beyond the mind, or none of them do. Put another way, the metaphysical status of the property of heat is an all-or-nothing affair – either all of the degrees of heat which we can experience objects to have are mind-dependent reactions in us, or they are all genuine features of material objects out there, independent of our perceptual reactions.

The second premise is that a very intense degree of heat *is one and the same thing* as a great pain, and that consequently, since pain can only exist in the mind of the subject who's experiencing it, the same must be true of a very intense degree of heat. Philonous then proceeds to apply the same line of thinking to less intense degrees of heat ('warmth') – a lesser degree of heat *is* one and the same thing as a feeling of pleasure, and hence a lesser degree of heat too can only exist in the mind of a perceiving subject.

And of course the implied conclusion that's taken to follow from these two premises is that *all* degrees of heat can only exist in the mind – that is, heat is a mind-dependent property.

Having dealt with the property of heat, Hylas subsequently concedes that the Identity Argument also proves that the various degrees of cold can only exist in the minds of perceiving subjects, for the same reasons – namely that the various degrees of cold we can experience objects to possess are themselves nothing other than sensations of pain or pleasure. Philonous then goes on to argue that sweetness is identical with feelings of pleasure, that bitterness is identical with 'uneasiness or pain', and that odours are identical with 'so many pleasing or displeasing sensations', each time with the conclusion that the properties in question are mind-dependent.

Hylas raises objections to the Identity Argument at a number of stages, to which Philonous responds. His first complaint is that rather than an intense degree of heat being one and the same thing as a sensation of pain, the intense degree of heat *causes*, and is in fact distinct from, the feeling of pain in question. Philonous responds that 'introspection' (the process whereby we review the contents of our own minds) reveals that there is just one 'simple and uncompounded' sensation in play when we experience an intense and painful degree of heat. Since we're directly aware of both the heat and the pain simultaneously, both the heat and the pain must be one and the same as this 'simple and uncompounded' sensation, and hence the heat and the pain must be identical with one another.

Hylas' next objection is that if we were to deny the first premise above which entails that if some degrees of heat are 'just in the mind' then the same is true for all degrees of heat, it need not follow from the identification of intense degrees of heat with feelings of pain that lesser degrees of heat are also nothing other than feelings of pleasure or pain. It's at this stage that Philonous states that lesser degrees of heat *are* identical with feelings of pleasure, with the usual conclusion that lesser degrees of heat are mind-dependent properties of objects. Hylas counters that there are some degrees of heat that are neither feelings of pain nor feelings of pleasure, and are exempt from the argument's force. At this point, Philonous does not persist with this Identity Argument, but moves on to present the Argument from Perceptual Relativity, which we'll examine presently in its turn. Before he goes on to do so though, he refers Hylas to 'his own sense' in order to convince him that it isn't the case that some lesser degrees of heat aren't identical with feelings of pleasure. It strikes me that what Philonous is doing in referring Hylas to 'his own sense' is again asking him to introspect and let what he finds when he examines the contents of his own mind settle the issue.

It's also worth noting the possible rejoinder to the Identity Argument that I earmarked earlier, as this potentially takes the form of a response to the objection that some degrees of heat are neither feelings of pain nor feelings of pleasure. On pp. 191–2 of the *Dialogues* Philonous attempts to explain the tendency of the philosophers of the day to maintain that Primary Qualities have 'real existence' (*i.e.*, they exist beyond the mind), and that Secondary Qualities do not. He suggests that this is because pleasure and pain are 'annexed' to the Secondary Qualities alone, and that 'heat and cold, taste and smells, have something more vividly pleasing or disagreeable' about them than do our perceptual experiences of the Primary Qualities. Philonous then claims that this explanation can be supported by considering that 'there is no rational ground', contrary to Hylas' suggestion, for allowing 'real existence' (*i.e.*, mind-independence) to less intense degrees of heat and denying it to more intense degrees. The reason he gives for this is that 'surely an indifferent sensation is as truly a *sensation*, as one more pleasing or painful'. What Philonous seems to be saying here is that it's still a *sensation* that we have when we feel an object to be hot but we feel neither pleasure nor pain in doing so.

Hylas' final objection to the Identity Argument is that it proves that an object's properties *as we experience them* can only exist in the mind, but it does not prove that the same is true for these properties *as they are in external objects*. In response, Philonous claims that this is an irrelevant objection, since all along they had only been considering the things we immediately perceive by sense (*i.e.*, the things we are aware of in the first instance when we perceive using our senses), rather than anything we go on to infer on the basis of what we immediately perceive. The clear implication, following the initial definitions agreed on by the two of them on pp. 174–5, is that it is only properties *as we experience them* that are to be counted among the things that we immediately perceive. Philonous concludes that the supposed properties *as they are in external objects* have got nothing to do with the Identity Argument, and he remarks that in fact he 'knows nothing of them'. (Recall here that Berkeley thinks that even on the materialists' account, we can't possibly know that there are mind-independent material objects and properties in existence beyond our own ideas – see above, pp. 96–7.)

Finally, as an aside, it's also important to record that in the middle of the passage containing the Identity Argument, Philonous introduces what looks like a *different* argument for the same conclusion (*i.e.*, that the properties we experience objects to have can only exist in the mind). He claims that Hylas can neither 'conceive a vehement sensation to be without pain or pleasure' (p. 176), nor 'frame [. . .] an idea of sensible pain or pleasure in general, abstracted from every particular idea of heat, cold, tastes, smells &c'. Hylas concedes on both counts, and also accepts Philonous' conclusion here that feelings of pain are not distinct from the intense degrees of the sensations of heat, cold *etc.* This argument, that an idea of pain/pleasure can't be abstracted from the ideas we have of heat/cold *etc.* and hence that feelings of pain/pleasure are identical with feelings of heat/cold, has exactly the same form as Berkeley's Argument from Conceptual Inseparability, which Philonous employs later in the *Dialogues* to try to prove that Primary Qualities can't exist beyond the mind (see below, pp. 163–5). The reason why it's important to record the occurrence of this argument here is that a number of Berkeley scholars claim that the Identity Argument *involves* Berkeley's denial of the possibility of abstract ideas, a denial which is key to the Argument from Conceptual Inseparability. However, I propose that the Identity Argument *doesn't* involve Berkeley's denial of the possibility of abstract ideas. Rather, I gather from the fact that the argument here has exactly the same form as the later Argument from Conceptual Inseparability, and a different form from the Identity Argument 'proper', that we have two distinct arguments in play in this passage of the text.

The Identity Argument – critical evaluation

I'm now going to run past you two of the main objections that commentators make to the Identity Argument, as well as suggesting to you what you might make of them. My own view, as you will see, is that ultimately the Identity Argument doesn't work. But its failure to prove that certain of an everyday object's properties *as we experience them* are sensations in our minds would have been no great loss for Berkeley, given that he provides us with further arguments for the conclusion that an everyday object's properties *anyhow defined* cannot possibly exist beyond the mind.

A first objection to the Identity Argument, and the one that receives most attention from commentators, is that we really should distinguish heat *as we experience it* and heat *as it is in objects*, and that this distinction entails the Identity Argument's demise. Even if it were the case that heat *as we experience it* is nothing other than a certain kind of sensation in us, this objection maintains that it still makes sense to talk about heat *as it is in objects* (such as the fire) being something other than a sensation in us.

In response to this objection, we've already seen that Berkeley himself anticipates this very claim in the course of presenting the Identity Argument, and that he has Philonous respond to it. Hylas complains (on p. 180) that this distinction should be drawn with respect to the properties that they have been considering, and Philonous replies that talking about these properties *as they exist in objects* is completely irrelevant, given that their discussion had been restricted all along to the things we immediately perceive by sense (*i.e.*, to properties *as we experience them*). It might seem at first then that this first objection that we're considering is also an irrelevant one to make.

However, there is some evidence that although Philonous claims that he's restricting the scope of the discussion to heat *as we experience it*, and ignoring for the moment heat *as it is in the fire*, Berkeley is in fact pulling a bit of a fast one. (See Kenneth Winkler's book *Berkeley: An Interpretation* for a similar expression of this kind of claim.) For although Philonous doesn't *explicitly* conclude in the course of the Identity Argument that there can be no heat *as it is in the fire* beyond our experiences of heat, there is something in the tenor of the Identity Argument itself that suggests that Berkeley is smuggling in the claim that the *only* kind of heat is heat *as we experience it*.

For one thing, on p. 175 of the *Dialogues*, right at the start of their discussion of heat, Philonous states that heat is a 'sensible thing' (*i.e.*, one of the things we are aware of when we perceive using our senses), and Hylas immediately agrees with him. But in fact on the previous page the two of them had defined 'sensible things' as those things *immediately* perceived by sense (*i.e.*, sensations). In which case, the thought that heat *anyhow defined* is a sensation in us has been smuggled in to the discussion before it has even really got going.

Later, on p. 177, Philonous follows up Hylas' concession that a 'very violent and painful heat cannot exist beyond the mind' by asking a rhetorical question: 'Is it therefore certain [on Hylas' account], that there is no body in nature really hot?' And, on p. 178, seizing on Hylas' admission that those degrees of heat which are pleasures and pains don't exist beyond the mind, Philonous asks again rhetorically: 'may we not conclude that external bodies are incapable of any degree of heat whatsoever?' On each occasion, if Hylas and Philonous are indeed restricting their discussion to heat *as we experience it*, Hylas could have answered Philonous by claiming that there *are* bodies in nature that really are hot, or that external bodies are capable of varying degrees of heat, so long as we are talking here about heat *as it is in objects*. The fact that Philonous is asking *rhetorical* questions which imply the answer that heat *anyhow defined* isn't a genuine property of objects out there beyond the mind (as they are in and of themselves, independent of our perceptual reactions to them) again suggests that Berkeley is surreptitiously doing away with the thought that heat *as it is in objects* might be distinct from heat *as we experience it*.

Finally, following Philonous' claim on p. 180 that all the while they have been discussing properties *as we experience them*, he asks Hylas afresh whether heat, cold, sweetness and bitterness exist beyond the mind (*stressing* that he means these properties *as we experience them*), and Hylas concedes that they don't. However, suddenly it seems that Hylas takes this conclusion to apply not just to these properties *as we experience them*, but to these properties *anyhow* defined. This emerges when he says straight away that he finds it strange 'to say that sugar is not sweet', a remark that Philonous doesn't comment on. But of course, if the most that the two of them have established was that sweetness *as we experience it* is a sensation in us, Hylas could still say that 'sugar is sweet', if by 'sweet' he's referring to sweetness *as it is in the sugar* (which presumably would be characterized in terms of the chemical properties of the sugar).

All in all, it looks as though Berkeley has indeed smuggled into the Identity Argument the thought that, for example, the only kind of heat is heat *as we experience it*, and it's this sleight of hand that allows his characters to conclude, for instance, that there is no sweetness *of any kind* in objects out there, and that sweetness anyhow defined is merely a sensation in us.

Be this as it may, even if we were to take Philonous at his word when he says that he is limiting the discussion to these various properties *as we experience them*, it becomes clear that the Identity Argument is nothing more than an argument for what in Berkeley's day was an uncontroversial conclusion. The conclusion would now be that heat, cold, tastes and odours *as we experience them* are sensations, and as such aren't genuine properties that material objects really do have, independent of our perceptual reactions to them. But in fact it was widely agreed on by philosophers in the seventeenth and eighteenth centuries that Secondary Qualities like these were indeed nothing other than sensations in our minds (see above, p. 47). So, it seems, Berkeley is caught in a dilemma. **Either** the Identity Argument (perhaps sneakily) concludes that heat and cold *etc. anyhow defined* are just sensations in our minds, in which case the objection remains that Berkeley fails to distinguish these properties *as we experience them* and *as they are in objects*. **Or** the Identity Argument concludes that heat and cold *etc. as we experience them* are just sensations in our minds, in which case the conclusion to the argument is one that was already widely accepted. Whichever way we turn, Berkeley still needs to present us with arguments for the conclusion that properties *anyhow defined* can't exist beyond the mind. As we'll see, this is something that he goes on to do, and we'll assess the further arguments that he gives us in due course.

The second objection to the Identity Argument that I want us to examine is more direct – it takes the form of a straight denial of the claim that heat *as we experience it* is identical with feelings of pleasure and pain. This is an objection again that Berkeley himself anticipates and responds to – he has Hylas claim that intense heat is distinct from, and in fact *causes*, the feelings of pain we get when we're too close to the fire. We saw above that Philonous responds by maintaining that introspection reveals to us that we have but one simple, uncompounded sensation when we experience a painfully intense heat, and so intense heat and the feeling of pain are indeed one and the same thing after all. But a number of commentators argue that it's questionable, if not downright false, that we have the simple, uncompounded sensation of pain/heat that Berkeley requires, at least in most cases when we experience painful or pleasant degrees of heat.

Try thinking about it this way. For one thing, it seems to me to be the case that sometimes we can experience an object to be hot without feeling any pleasure or pain whatsoever. If that's right, then it looks (at least at first) as though we might have found a counter-example to Berkeley's claim that *all* degrees of heat *as we experience it* are identical with some feeling of pleasure/pain or other. As we've seen, Berkeley himself in effect provides a reply to this claim when he has Philonous state, albeit in a different context, that 'surely an indifferent sensation is as truly a *sensation*, as one more pleasing or painful'. Again what Philonous seems to be saying here is that it's still a *sensation* that we have when we feel an object to be hot but we feel neither pleasure nor pain in doing so. But this reply won't do, because Berkeley presents the Identity Argument in an attempt to *prove* that properties like heat are in fact identical with sensations. Surely it's no good trying to defend the Identity Argument against criticism by trotting out the very claim that the argument is designed to establish, in *asserting* that a feeling of heat that's neither painful nor pleasurable is a sensation nonetheless.

Perhaps Berkeley's already done enough though, *before* he points out that an indifferent sensation is still a sensation nevertheless, to establish that all degrees of heat are in fact sensations. After all, the first premise of the argument entails that if one degree of heat is a sensation that's just in the mind then the same is true of all degrees of heat. And the second premise is that a very intense heat *is* a sensation of pain that's just in the mind. On the assumption that these two premises are true, it follows that all degrees of heat, including those that are neither painful nor pleasurable, are indeed sensations that are just in the mind. A relevant question to ask here then is whether or not it *is* true that a very intense heat is one and the same thing as a sensation of pain. Various commentators have argued in different ways why this in fact *isn't* true, and I'll leave you with just one thing to think about under this head. Take the sensation you're aware of when you burn your hand on the stove. Is it true to say that this sensation of pain is one and the same thing as the property of extreme heat? One reason to think that it this is not the case is that you can have the self-same sensation of pain when you experience an ice burn – for instance if you're unlucky enough to handle an extremely cold piece of metal. Here, Berkeley would be bound to say that the sensation of pain in question is not only identical with the property of extreme heat, but it's also one and the same thing as the property of extreme cold. But then, by what philosophers call 'the transitivity of identity' (according to which, if *a* is identical to *b*, and *b* is identical to *c*, then *a* is identical to *c*), he would be committed to the claim that the property of extreme heat is one and the same thing as the property of extreme cold. But that's absurd, isn't it? If it is, then this seems like a good reason for us not to accept Berkeley's Identity Argument – it has daft consequences like this one.

What do you make of these objections? Are you persuaded by either of them? Or do you think that Berkeley's Identity Argument can be defended against them? Have a think about it, bearing in mind what Berkeley actually says in the text, and perhaps have a read of what other people have to say about the Identity Argument, to help yourself to some further food-for-thought.

iv. THE ARGUMENT FROM PERCEPTUAL RELATIVITY

The Argument from Perceptual Relativity occurs briefly in the *Principles*, and at greater length in the *Dialogues*. In fact, Berkeley presents us with *three* different versions of the argument, all of which proceed from the premise that the properties we experience everyday objects to have vary from person to person, or from one set of perceptual circumstances to another. His typical conclusion is that the 'sensible qualities' (*i.e.*, the properties we experience everyday objects to have when we perceive using our senses) are sensations. In other words, The Argument from Perceptual

Relativity is another attempt on Berkeley's part to *prove* by way of argument that one of the claims that he simply *asserts* at the start of the *Dialogues* and the main body of the *Principles* is indeed true.

As a quick aside, be aware that some Berkeley scholars argue that he *doesn't* introduce the Argument from Perceptual Relativity in order to defend his own view that 'sensible qualities' are merely sensations in us. Rather, they maintain that he only ever uses it to argue *ad hominem* against people who think that it's the case, or perhaps that we can *know* that it's the case, that the properties we experience everyday objects to have are genuine properties that material objects really do have in and of themselves, independent of our perceptual reactions to them. (Roughly speaking, to argue *ad hominem* against someone is to argue against them on their own terms, for example by turning their own arguments against them in the attempt to show that their position or theory *etc.* is flawed). For our purposes here, I'm simply going to state that I think that this reading of the argument is mistaken, and that Berkeley does indeed use it on various occasions to establish not just that his opponent's claims are mistaken but also that his own claims are in fact true. Nonetheless, it's worth asking yourself what you think Berkeley is up to when you read the passages in the *Principles* and the *Dialogues* in which he present the various versions of the Argument from Perceptual Relativity.

The three versions of the argument

The first version occurs, with minor variations, at §§14–15 and §87 of the *Principles* (with reference to *all* of the 'sensible qualities'), and in the *Dialogues* on pp. 185–6 (with reference to colour) and pp. 205–6 (with reference again to all 'sensible qualities'). In this version, Berkeley's first premise is that one and the same everyday object will seem to have (say) a different size or colour to different people, or that one and the same object will seem to a single person to have a different size or colour in different perceptual circumstances. So, for instance, a tower may look small to someone a long way away from it, but much larger to someone stood right next to it, and, to use one of Berkeley's own examples, an object that normally tastes sweet might taste bitter to someone who has a fever. His second premise is that the different properties that various people experience one and the same object to have, or that one person experiences one and the same object to have in different perceptual circumstances, can't *all* be representative of the genuine, mind-independent properties that object is supposed to have in and of itself, out there beyond our minds. For instance, one and the same material object out there can't *actually* be large *and* small, or bitter *and* sweet, independent of our perceptual experiences of the object in question.

From these two premises, Berkeley sometimes draws the conclusion that *none* of our perceptual experiences actually represent the genuine, mind-independent properties that objects are supposed to have in and of themselves, out there beyond our minds. In the *Principles* however, he draws a different conclusion – namely that we can't *know* which, if any, of our perceptual experiences represent the true properties of the supposed mind-independent material objects. Indeed in one place (§15 of the *Principles*), having provisionally reached the former conclusion, he back-tracks and says that the most the argument can prove is the latter conclusion. The reason for this back-tracking here seems to be that Berkeley *does* present the argument in the *Principles* merely as an *ad hominem* device against the materialists, using their own arguments against them. As I noted back in Chapter 2, philosophers in the seventeenth and eighteenth centuries often appealed to 'perceptual relativity' in arguing that the Secondary Qualities such as the colour, heat, taste and smell that we experience objects to have weren't genuine, mind-independent properties of material objects out there, but were rather merely features of our own perceptual reactions (see above, p. 47). In §§14–15 of the *Principles*, Berkeley notes that this argument of the 'modern philosophers' could equally apply to the Primary Qualities too, before pointing out that their argument as it stands is invalid, and that the most it could prove is that we can't know which, if any, of the properties we experience an object to have represent its true properties. Ultimately though Berkeley thinks that his opponents' argument here can in fact be adapted in such a way that it does prove that *none* of the properties we experience objects to have represent genuine, mind-independent properties of material objects. We'll come back to quite how he does this in a short while (see below, p. 156–7).

The second version of the Argument from Perceptual Relativity occurs, again with minor variations, in the *Dialogues* on pp. 178–9 (with reference to heat and cold), pp. 184–5 (colour), pp. 188–9 (extension and figure) and p. 190 (motion). The argument this time takes the form of what philosophers call a '*reductio ad absurdum* proof' that the claim that mind-independent material objects really do have the properties that we experience them to have is in fact false. (In a *reductio ad absurdum* proof, we are literally reducing a given claim to absurdity. The method is that, having assumed for the sake of argument that a given set of claims are all true (including the claim that we want to debunk), we proceed to prove that it's possible to derive a contradiction (an 'absurdity') from the set of claims in question. It's a rule of logic that a set of claims which are all true can't entail a contradiction, so we know, having derived our contradiction, that at least one of the original claims whose truth we assumed for the sake of argument is in fact false. We then put to one side the original claims that actually are true, which will leave us with the target claim that we've proven to be false.)

So, Berkeley runs for the sake of argument with the claim that mind-independent material objects really do have the properties that we experience them to have. He then notes that we can simultaneously experience one and the same object to have different degrees of a given property. One of his own examples here is that one and the same body of water can simultaneously feel hot to one hand and cold to the other. (You can find this out for yourself if you like. Warm up one of your hands (say by putting in a glove for a minute or two) and cool the other one down (say by immersing it for a while in a sink of cold water). Then put both of your hands (having removed the glove) into a bath of lukewarm water. You'll find that the water in the bath feels warm to one hand and cold to the other.) But if it were true (so this version of the Argument from Perceptual Relativity goes) that mind-independent material objects really do have the properties we experience them to have, then it would follow that, for example, the water in the bath really is both hot and cold at the same time, independent of our perceptual reactions to it, which is absurd. So we know that it's not true that mind-independent material objects really do have the properties that we experience them to have. The properties that we experience objects to have must be something other than genuine, mind-independent properties of the objects in question. Berkeley's view of course is that they are in fact just sensations in us.

The third version of the Argument from Perceptual Relativity occurs, once again with minor variations, in the *Dialogues* on pp. 185–6 (with reference to colour) and on p. 189 (with reference to 'visible extension' – that is, the extent to which we experience an object to be 'spread out' when we look at it). The first premise this time is the materialists' claim that a genuine, mind-independent property of a material object can only change as a result of a change to the object itself. (The thought here is that we can only change an object's shape, for instance, by doing something to the object – say by hitting it with a hammer.) The second premise is that an object's 'sensible qualities' *can* change *without* there having been a change in the object we experience them to be properties of. To use another of Berkeley's own examples, the colour that we experience an object to be in daylight will change if we view it now by candlelight, despite the fact that the object itself hasn't changed one bit. Given that a material object's genuine, mind-independent properties can change only if the object itself changes, and given that the properties we experience objects to have can change without a change in the object itself, this version of the argument's conclusion is that the properties we experience objects to have can't be genuine, mind-independent properties of material objects. Again, Berkeley's own view is that they are in fact just sensations in us.

In summary, in each version of the Argument from Perceptual Relativity Berkeley (or Philonous) argues from the fact that different observers can perceive one and the same object to have different properties, or that a single observer can perceive one and the same object to have different properties in different perceptual circumstances, to the conclusion that the properties that we experience objects to have are *not* mind-*independent* properties of those objects. This conclusion is equivalent to the claim that the properties we experience objects to have are mind-*dependent* properties of those objects, and hence we find Berkeley maintaining that the properties we experience objects to have are indeed all mind-*dependent* properties at various places in both the *Principles* and the *Dialogues*. And like many of his contemporary philosophers in the seventeenth and eighteenth centuries, Berkeley characterizes the properties of objects that turn out to be mind-dependent features of our own perceptual experiences as being *sensations*.

The Argument From Perceptual Relativity – critical evaluation

Let's take a look at a couple of common objections to the Argument from Perceptual Relativity. I'm going to suggest to you that the first of these objections can provisionally be overcome. And I think that the second objection can also be countered, but only at a cost. In fact Berkeley himself responds to the second objection, yet when we examine how he goes about doing so, we'll see that he renders his own Argument from Perceptual Relativity trivial, redundant and circular.

The first objection applies specifically to the first version of the argument, and it takes the form of the claim that while not *all* of our perceptual experiences of an object's properties can represent the genuine, mind-independent properties that the object really does have, it doesn't follow that *none* of them do, or that we can't know *which* of them do. Recall Berkeley's example whereby an object which I normally experience as being sweet tastes bitter to me when I've got a fever. Which of my perceptual experiences reveals the one, true taste of the object in question? Berkeley's claim is that the fact that I experience a different taste on each occasion shows that neither experience reveals the one, true taste of the object, or at least that I can't know which of them does so.

But that's not right, is it? Surely it's the case that the sweet taste that I normally experience is the one, true taste of the object, and indeed that I know that this is the case. This is because I know that when I have a fever, my sense of taste isn't working properly – in this instance, the perceptual circumstances that I'm in are *abnormal*. It's when the perceptual circumstances that I'm in are *normal* that

I can be confident that my senses reveal to me the true properties of the objects I perceive. Likewise, when two observers experience one and the same object to have a different colour or a different shape, for example, we can often easily identify which of the observers is perceiving the object in normal perceptual circumstances, and hence which of them has perceptual experiences that reveal the object's one, true colour or shape. To use a couple of examples of my own, suppose that a person with normal colour vision sees a strawberry as being red, whereas another person who is colour blind sees it as being brown. Or suppose that someone who is sober sees a wall as being stationary and as having a flat surface, whereas it seems to someone else who is blind drunk that the wall is moving and has a wibbly-wobbly surface. In each case, we typically take it to be an extremely simple task to decide which of them has a perceptual experience which reveals the one, true colour or shape of the object in question – again by noting which of them interacts with the object in normal perceptual circumstances.

But there are in fact a number of things that Berkeley has his characters say in the *Dialogues* discussion of the Argument from Perceptual Relativity that might give us the means to defend his argument against this particular objection. Specifically, Philonous sometimes talks in a way which suggests that there is after all no good reason to think the perceptual experiences *we* have in what *we* deem to be normal perceptual circumstances are the ones which reveal to us the genuine, mind-independent properties of everyday objects. To give just one example, on pp. 188–9 of the *Dialogues*, Philonous gets Hylas to concede that members of other species of animal would have just as good reason as we do to think (if indeed they think at all) that the size and shape they experience objects to be are the one, true mind-independent size and shape of the objects in question. But of course, Philonous goes on to note, objects that seem to be tiny to us will seem huge to creatures smaller than mites. So which of us – humans or creatures smaller than mites – has perceptual experiences which reveal the one, true size of things? What Philonous is implying in this passage, I think, is that it's merely *biased* thinking for us to suppose that it's our *own* species' normal perceptual experiences that do so. Given the differences in the ways everyday objects typically appear to the members of different species, perhaps the most we can conclude on the basis of our own perceptual experiences is that in what *human beings* call normal perceptual circumstances, a given object will typically look big *to human beings*, for example.

And if ultimately there is no good reason for thinking that any one species' perceptual experiences (in what *for that species* are normal perceptual circumstances) reveal an object's genuine, mind-independent size, shape and colour *etc.*, then perhaps Berkeley's conclusion that *none* of our perceptual experiences do so can be justified after all. Because if there's no good reason for concluding that any *one* species' perceptual experiences reveal an object's genuine, mind-independent properties, there is at least the threat that there is no good reason to suppose that *any* species' perceptual experiences do so. (N.B. Kenneth P. Winkler also suggests that the Argument from Perceptual Relativity can be strengthened in this kind of way in his book *Berkeley: An Interpretation*.)

This particular debate doesn't end here though. Whether or not there ultimately are good reasons for concluding that we can know that the perceptual experiences that human beings have in normal perceptual circumstances do in fact reveal the genuine, mind-independent properties of everyday objects is something for you to think about further.

The second common objection that I want to examine applies either directly or indirectly to all three versions of the Argument from Perceptual Relativity, but most obviously to the third version, and it's a criticism that we've seen before in another context (see above, pp. 145f.). It's the claim that Berkeley fails to distinguish between an object's properties *as we experience them* and *as they are in the object*, and that once we draw this distinction his argument simply doesn't go through. Recall how the third version of the Argument from Perceptual Relativity relies on the premise that an object's 'sensible qualities' *can* change even though the object itself hasn't changed one bit. But, various commentators note, the materialist could simply deny that this is the case. It's true that (for example) the size, shape and colour that we experience an object to have (its properties *as we experience them*) can change even though the object hasn't. But it doesn't follow from this fact alone that the object's actual properties (its properties *as they are in the object*) have also changed. For example, many people would take it to be the case that a red object is still red, even when it looks to us to be orange when we look at it by candlelight, or that a large object is still large, even when it looks small to us when we view it through a telescope held the wrong way round. And without the crucial claim that an object's properties *anyhow defined* can change without the object changing, the third version of the Argument from Perceptual Relativity doesn't even get off the ground.

Just as he did when presenting the Identity Argument though, Berkeley himself again anticipates and has Philonous respond to this very objection that he has failed to distinguish between 'sensible qualities' *as we experience them* and *as they are in objects*. In fact, Philonous considers a number of forms of this objection, and I want to spend a little time examining the main ones in turn. The first (on p. 191 of the *Dialogues*) sees Hylas wanting to distinguish what we *immediately* perceive when we perceive a given property (which he concedes is *not* a genuine, mind-independent property of an object) from the *cause* of our immediate perceptual experience (which is). Philonous responds on this occasion that their discussion all along was restricted to a consideration of the things we *immediately* perceive, and that the *causes* of our immediate perceptual experiences are not themselves immediately perceived, and are therefore irrelevant to the point in hand.

Soon after, on p. 192, Hylas proposes that we should distinguish between 'absolute qualities' and 'sensible qualities'. He contends that 'sensible qualities', such as 'great and small' *are* merely features of our own perceptual reactions to objects, but that 'absolute qualities' are not. In other words, 'sensible qualities' are an object's properties *as we experience them*, which are distinct from 'absolute qualities' or properties *as they are in objects*. In response, Philonous claims (on p. 193) that the very concept of these 'absolute qualities' existing distinct from (or 'abstracted from') 'sensible qualities' is one of the unacceptably abstract ideas that Berkeley rejects elsewhere. On Berkeley's (and Philonous') account, we can't even conceive of the possibility of an 'absolute quality' (a property *as it is in the object*) that's distinct from a 'sensible quality' (a property *as we experience it*). And since 'absolute qualities' are conceptually impossible, Philonous can't be guilty of failing to distinguish between properties *as we experience them* and properties *as they are in objects*.

Finally, Hylas suggests (on p. 195) that there's a distinction to be drawn between a quality considered as a *sensation* (which can't exist beyond the mind) and the 'object' of this sensation – that is, the thing that the sensation represents (which can and does exist beyond the mind). Philonous this time persuades Hylas to admit that this 'object' itself can only be something we immediately perceive, and hence is itself a sensation. Consequently, Philonous again concludes that there is no distinction to be drawn between qualities considered as sensations (*i.e.*, properties *as we experience them*) and the supposed qualities *as they are in objects*.

Each of these responses has unfortunate implications for the fate of the Argument from Perceptual Relativity, however. If, following the first response, we accept that the Argument from Perceptual Relativity was only ever intended to apply to our *immediate* perceptual experiences of an object's properties – that is, to the properties we experience an object to have *in the first instance* when we perceive using our senses – then the argument turns out to be a trivial one. As we saw in Chapter 3, Berkeley sometimes defines the things we immediately perceive as those things we're aware of in the first instance when we perceive using our senses, *before* the mind jumps to consider any further ideas on the basis of what we immediately perceive (see above, pp. 69–70). Considered in this sense, it *is* the case, for example, that two observers stood at different distances from a tower each see a tower of a different size (even if they both subsequently judge, say, that it's a big tower) – but only in the sense, say, that the image of the tower takes up a far larger proportion of the visual field of one observer than it does of that of another. Similarly, one and the same object looms large in a mite's visual field (given Berkeley's assumption on p. 186 of the *Dialogues* that mites don't go around 'stark blind') but only barely registers in our own. So the conclusion to the Argument from Perceptual Relativity, if it's only intended to apply to our *immediate* perceptual experiences of an object's properties, amounts to nothing more than the claim that properties like 'taking up a large proportion of a mite's visual field', or 'taking up a small proportion of my own my visual field' are not genuine, mind-independent properties of objects. That is, the Argument from Perceptual Relativity turns out to be an argument for a *trivial* conclusion. One obvious remark to make here would be that no one ever thought that *these* sorts of properties *were* genuine, mind-independent properties of objects. Another would be that this conclusion alone by itself clearly doesn't justify the further conclusion that an object's properties *anyhow considered* are not genuine, mind-independent properties of a material object out there in the world beyond our minds.

Meanwhile, when Berkeley has Philonous claim that it's conceptually impossible that there should be 'absolute qualities' (*i.e.*, properties *as they are in objects*) independent from or 'abstracted' from 'sensible qualities' (*i.e.*, properties *as we experience them*), he's trying to save the Argument from Perceptual Relativity by appealing to further arguments he gives us against the possibility of abstract ideas. That is, the success of the Argument from Perceptual Relativity depends on the success of Berkeley's arguments against abstract ideas. We'll be examining these arguments themselves in a moment (see below, specifically pp. 167–9). But for now, let's just note that one of the conclusions that Berkeley draws from his arguments against abstract ideas is that there can be no such thing as mind-independent properties of objects. This being the case, there's really *no need* for him to present a separate argument (the Argument from Perceptual Relativity) for the conclusion that the properties we experience everyday objects to have are not genuine, mind-independent properties of objects, given that this argument's success depends on the success of other arguments for the same conclusion. In other words, this particular response to the original objection that Berkeley fails to distinguish properties *as we experience them* and properties *as they are in objects* renders the Argument from Perceptual Relativity *redundant*.

And what of Philonous' third response to this objection, that there is in fact no distinction to be drawn between the properties of objects considered as sensations in our minds and the properties of objects considered as the things that those sensations represent or tell us about? The question to ask at this point is this: whoever said that an object's properties *as we experience them* were just sensations in our minds? In fact, wasn't the Argument from Perceptual Relativity supposed to be an argument for the *conclusion* that the 'sensible qualities' are sensations? If so, then here Berkeley has used the very claim the argument is supposed to establish to defend the argument against criticism, and in doing so he's arguing in a circle. Only someone who *already* accepts that the 'sensible qualities' are just sensations in our minds will be persuaded that the Argument from Perceptual Relativity can be defended from criticism in this way. Philonous' third response to the original objection ab. will be no good to anyone who doesn't *already* accept the conclusion that Berkeley is trying to persuade us to agree with in presenting the Argument from Perceptual Relativity.

In short, the three responses that Philonous makes to the objection that he (and thus Berkeley) fails to distinguish between an object's properties *as we experience them* and those properties *as they are in the object* show that the Argument for Perceptual Relativity is alternatively trivial, redundant and circular. If this is right, then the Argument from Perceptual Relativity fails to establish that the various properties we experience everyday objects to have aren't genuine, mind-independent properties of objects but are rather just sensations in our minds.

v. BERKELEY'S ARGUMENTS AGAINST ABSTRACT IDEAS

In this final section we're going to consider what are traditionally taken to be Berkeley's more advanced moves in his attempt to prove that there can be no such thing as everyday objects, their properties, or indeed matter itself existing beyond the mind. These are the moves which involve his famous attack on the claim that we can entertain (or 'frame') *abstract general ideas* of various kinds (often simply called 'abstract ideas' for short). It's often thought that in arguing that we can't possibly entertain these kinds of ideas, Berkeley is specifically attacking John Locke's account of abstract ideas, and indeed it's clear that Berkeley often has what he takes to be Locke's view in his sights here. (For a general overview of Locke's philosophy, see above, pp. 37–41.) However, there is some debate these days about what Locke's account of abstract ideas actually was, and some commentators argue that Berkeley in fact misinterprets Locke's view and ends up attacking an account of abstract ideas that Locke never held. For the record, I don't think that Berkeley did misinterpret Locke in this way; and in fact it's irrelevant for our purposes whether he did so or not. This is because he still presents us with *an* attack on the possibility of abstract ideas, and consequently with arguments for the conclusion that everyday objects, their properties, or indeed matter itself can't possibly exist beyond the mind. This attack and these arguments remain whether he misinterpreted *Locke* or not.

There's also disagreement among Berkeley scholars concerning how many distinct kinds of abstract idea Berkeley took exception to. There are two kinds that pretty much everyone agrees he attacked. The first of these is ideas whose content is supposed to feature a single property (such as a shape) in isolation from all other properties (such as a colour). The second is ideas whose content is supposed to include all of the features that the different members of a given class of things have in common, but doesn't include those features that mark the different members of that class apart from one another. We're going to take a look at Berkeley's reasons for rejecting both of these kinds of idea, as well as the arguments he subsequently bases on their demise. In the process we'll also encounter his claim that the very idea of a mind-independent property, a material object, or indeed matter, is itself an unacceptably abstract idea which should be rejected in its turn.

Ideas whose content features a single property in isolation from all other properties

Berkeley takes exception to the claim that we can entertain or frame ideas whose content features a single property in isolation from all other properties. (See, *e.g.*, §7 and §10 of the Introduction to the *Principles* and pp. 193–4 of the *Dialogues*.) What he's claiming here is that (for instance) we can't frame an idea of a given *colour* that isn't also an idea of a given degree of *extension* (*i.e.*, the property of being spread out). Nor can we frame an idea of a given extension that isn't also an idea of a given colour (or some other equivalent Secondary Quality, such as a given 'feel'). For example, he takes it to be the case that any idea we have of a given colour will be an idea of a *patch* of that colour that's spread out this way and that; and any idea we have of something that's spread out this way and that will be an idea of a given expanse of colour or a given expanse of 'feels' *etc.* In trying to justify these claims, Berkeley remarks that everyone accepts that properties such as colour and extension can't exist in isolation from one another *in reality*, and that it's impossible for us to separate *in our thoughts* properties which can't exist in isolation from one another in reality. Here, he's claiming that *because* in reality colours are always spread out in extended patches and *because* extended patches are always patches of (for instance) colour, we can't conceive of these properties existing in isolation from one another in our thoughts.

He also offers us what appears at first to be a psychological challenge here – simply inspecting the contents of our own minds will confirm to us that we can't in fact frame this kind of abstract idea. He's supremely confident, for example, that any idea of a colour that we entertain will also be an idea of a particular expanse or extension of that colour, and that any idea of extension that we have will also be an idea of some colour or 'feel' or so on of which it *is* an extension or expanse. As many commentators note though, if this challenge is merely a psychological one, and Berkeley is hoping to prove that there can be no abstract ideas of this kind simply on the basis that an inspection of the contents of our own minds will reveal that there aren't any, then his case is particularly weak. It would only require someone to report that, yes, they had discovered an abstract idea of this kind in his or her mind for Berkeley's argument to fail. However, given that he ultimately argues that it's *impossible* that there could be such abstract ideas, it's highly likely that Berkeley makes his challenge confident in his opinion that we'll never find any when we inspect the contents of our minds.

The Argument From Conceptual Inseparability

Berkeley then puts to use the claim that we can't frame this kind of abstract idea as a premise in what's often called the Argument from Conceptual Inseparability. (See §10 and §99 of Part I of the *Principles* and p. 194 and p. 200 of the *Dialogues*.) The conclusion of this argument is that the Primary Qualities, such as the property of extension (*i.e.*, being spread out), the property of shape and the property of motion, can't exist beyond the mind. These are *mind-dependent* properties that are essentially features of our own perceptual experiences, rather than genuine, mind-independent properties of material objects out there beyond our minds.

The *Principles* version of the argument runs as follows. Because a person can't even *think* of a Primary Quality like extension without also thinking of a Secondary Quality like colour (the two being *conceptually inseparable*), we know that the property of extension, like the property of colour, can't exist beyond the mind. (Recall that it was widely accepted by philosophers in Berkeley's day that the Secondary Qualities such as colour were mind-dependent reactions in us, rather than mind-independent properties of material objects out there beyond the mind – see above, p. 47. We've seen too how Berkeley has tried to argue that what other people called the Secondary Qualities are just sensations in our minds.) What Berkeley is driving at with the *Principles* version of the Argument from Conceptual Inseparability is something like this – to think of the property of extension is to think of a mind-dependent property (like colour). The very idea or concept of the property of extension is the concept of a property that's inextricably bound up with something that's mind-dependent (such as the property of colour) – and therefore the concept of the property of extension is the concept of a property that's inextricably bound up with the mind. That's just to say, the very concept of the property of extension is itself the concept of a mind-dependent property.

In the *Dialogues* version meanwhile, Philonous forces Hylas to agree that it's impossible for something which 'implies a repugnancy in its conception' to actually exist. Philonous then goes on to argue that since it's impossible to frame an idea of the property of extension or of the property of motion in isolation from 'all other sensible qualities', it's necessarily the case that the properties of extension and motion can't exist independent of 'all other sensible qualities' in reality. The agreed conclusion is again that the *conceptual* inseparability of Primary Qualities and Secondary Qualities (*i.e.*, their inseparability in our thoughts, or in the contents of our ideas) means that they are *both* mind-dependent. Again what Berkeley (via Philonous) has in mind here is that because it's impossible to conceive of a property like extension without invoking mind-dependent considerations (such as the mind-dependent property of colour), then the property of extension can't exist independent from mind-dependent considerations in reality. Or in other words, Primary Qualities like extension in reality are mind-dependent properties.

It's worth emphasising what at first might strike you as a puzzling feature of Berkeley's attack on abstract ideas which crops up here and elsewhere. We've seen him claiming in the first place that what can't possibly be the case *in reality* can't possibly be the case *in our thoughts*. (Specifically, we've seen him claiming that because a property like extension and a property like colour can't exist in isolation from one another in reality, we can't even conceive of them existing in isolation from one another in our thoughts – see above, pp. 162–3.) But then, in the *Dialogues* version of the Argument from Conceptual Inseparability, he claimed conversely that what we can't possibly conceive of *in our thoughts* can't possibly be the case *in reality*. (Again, specifically he claimed that because we can't even conceive of a property like extension and a property like colour existing in isolation from one another, they can't possibly exist in isolation from one another in reality). Which is it to be, you might well ask? Does a given state of affairs' *impossibility* entail its *inconceivability*, or does its *inconceivability* entail its *impossibility*? We'll return to this question in due course.

Ideas whose content includes only those features common to all members of a given class of things

The second kind of abstract idea that Berkeley rejects is one whose content is supposed to include all of the features that the different members of a given class of things have in common, but doesn't include those features that mark the different members of that class apart from one another. (See §§8–10 of the Introduction to the *Principles* for an early description of this kind of abstract idea.) Here are a couple of Berkeley's own examples. The abstract idea of a triangle is supposed to be the idea of something which has three sides and three internal angles adding up to 180° (because all triangles do), but which is neither an equilateral triangle, nor a right-angled triangle, nor an isosceles triangle *etc.* (because not all triangles are equilateral, not all triangles are right-angled and not all triangles are isosceles *etc.*). Or take the supposed abstract idea of the property of colour – according to Berkeley, this would have to be an idea of a colour of *some* shade or other (because all colours are colours of *some* shade or other) but it won't be an idea of *red*, or *white*, or *green*, or of any determinate shade (because there's no one determinate shade that all colours have in common).

Berkeley denies that we can frame this kind of abstract idea for what at first look like two different reasons. On the one hand, his complaint is that it's impossible for us to do so. So he denies that we can frame an idea of a triangle that's neither an equilateral triangle, nor a right-angled triangle, nor an isosceles triangle *etc.*, because to do so is to try to frame an idea of a triangle that's *no* kind of triangle, which is impossible. Likewise, he denies that we can frame an idea of the property of colour that's an idea neither of the colour red, nor the colour white, nor the colour black, nor any other particular determinate colour whatsoever. Again to do so is to try to think of a colour that isn't any colour at all – another impossibility. On the other hand, the problem that Berkeley sometimes seems to have with these ideas is that they turn out to be ideas of *nothing at all* – non-ideas that are devoid of any content whatsoever. An idea that's supposed to be an idea of a triangle but that's not an idea of this, that or the other particular kind of triangle isn't an idea of anything, is it? Or an idea that's supposed to be an idea of the property of colour but that is an idea neither of the colour red, nor the colour white, nor the colour black and so on – surely that's not an idea of anything at all either. At least that's what Berkeley claims. And he's so confident that we can't entertain these kinds of ideas that he keeps challenging us to do so – just try to come up with an idea of an object's colour that's the idea of neither a red colour, nor a black colour, nor a white colour *etc.*, and you'll soon find that you can't, he says.

We can't even conceive of properties, everyday objects, or matter existing beyond the mind

Consequently, Berkeley applies his rejection of this kind of abstract idea in various arguments which are designed to prove that there can in fact be no such thing as a property, an everyday object, or indeed matter, existing beyond the mind. That said, it's difficult to provide helpful references that pin down single passages in which he presents these arguments. This is because he slowly builds up his case (primarily) over the course of the first half of Part I of the *Principles* and in the First Dialogue in the *Dialogues*. Nonetheless, here is a sample of references that you might find useful. For his argument that the properties of everyday objects can't exist beyond the mind, see, *e.g., Principles* §11 and *Dialogues* pp. 192–4. For something approaching a snapshot statement of his argument that everyday objects and/or matter itself can't exist beyond the mind, see *Principles* §§15–17, 47 and 73 and *Dialogues* p. 260.

Let's start with Primary Qualities – an object's size, for example. The very idea of size being a genuine, mind-independent property of material objects out there beyond the mind is a non-starter, Berkeley claims. The concept of size as a mind-independent property of material objects is supposed to be the concept of size as it is in and of itself out there in the external world, independent of any considerations that make essential reference to our minds. Or to put it another way, here we're trying to conceive of what an object's size would be like were there no minds in existence to perceive it. So we need to discard from our concept of mind-independent size any mind-dependent features of the property. But, says Berkeley, once we do this we'll find that there's nothing left for us to have an idea *of*. The supposed idea of mind-independent size turns out to be an *empty* idea, an idea with no content, an idea of *nothing* – which is the same as saying that it's no idea at all, or that we can have no such idea. People who claim that there is such a thing as the mind-independent size that an object has out there in the world beyond us *quite literally* have no idea what they are talking about.

To go into a little bit more detail, Berkeley argues that all particular 'determinations' of size are in fact mind-dependent considerations – they are all features of our perceptual experiences which make essential reference to us and our minds. What we mean when we say that an object is big, for example, is that it is big *relative to us*. After all (and to use my own examples), the same thing that we take to be big, a brontosaurus may well take to be small. Likewise, what we mean when we say that an object is small is that it is small *relative to us* – one and the same object can be small as far as we are concerned but big as far as a flea is concerned. And so too for all the other particular determinations of size (huge, tiny, medium-sized *etc.*) – these are all features of objects that are everything to do with us and our perceptual experiences of an object's properties, and nothing to do with the way an object's properties really are in and of themselves out there beyond the mind, independent of us. So the size that an object is supposed to have independent of us and our perceptual experiences will be neither big, nor small, nor huge, nor tiny, nor medium-sized *etc.* There's no determinate size that we can have in mind when we try to frame an idea of an object's mind-independent size – we're literally thinking of nothing at all. Hence, Berkeley concludes that the very idea of size being a mind-independent property of material objects out there beyond the mind is an idea with no content, an empty idea, a non-idea. Instead, whenever we think of an object's size, we must be thinking of a property that's merely a feature of our own perceptual experiences of that object – a property that necessarily finds its home among the perceptual ideas that we have when we perceive that object using our senses.

And Berkeley thinks that what we've just seen with regard to the property of size applies to *all* of an object's so-called Primary Qualities. To give just one further example, the very idea of the property of *motion* that a material object is supposed to have beyond the mind also turns out to be an empty idea and thus a non-idea. Fast, slow, medium-paced and indeed all other determinate degrees of motion are everything to do with us and the perceptual ideas that we have when we experience moving objects, and nothing to do with the way material objects are out there beyond our minds. To use my own example, what we take to be a fast-moving object, a fly may well take to be a slow-moving object and so on. So again the mind-independent motion that an object is supposed to have turns out to be neither fast, nor slow, nor-medium-paced, nor any other determinate degree of motion. There's no determinate degree of motion that we can have in mind when we're trying to frame the idea of an object's mind-independent motion, which is to say that we're thinking of nothing at all when we try to do so. Once more, people who claim that there's such a thing as the mind-independent motion of objects literally have no idea what they're talking about. Any mention of an object's motion necessarily involves reference to us and the perceptual ideas our minds entertain – and thus motion is a *mind-dependent* property.

The position Berkeley thinks he's reached here is that *all* of the properties of everyday objects are mind-dependent properties, having everything to do with us and our perceptual experiences, and nothing to do with the way material objects are supposed to be out there beyond the mind, independent of us. We've just seen that he's established (at least to his own satisfaction) that all of the so-called Primary Qualities are mind-dependent properties of objects, and we've seen previously that he thinks that he's proved the same for the so-called Secondary Qualities (for example, with the Argument from Perceptual Relativity). From this position, Berkeley takes just a short step to the further conclusion that there can be no such thing as a mind-independent material object, or indeed mind-independent matter.

Again, according to him, the very idea that there could be such a thing as a mind-independent material object turns out to be an idea that's devoid of content – an empty idea or non-idea. The would-be idea or concept of a mind-independent material object is supposed to be the idea of a material object as it is in and of itself out there in the external world, independent of any considerations that make essential reference to our minds. So once more we need to remove from our idea of a mind-independent material object any mind-dependent properties or features of that object. But since *all* of the properties that we experience objects to have are mind-dependent properties (because both the so-called Primary and Secondary Qualities alike are mind-dependent properties), once we've done this we're left with an idea of something that has no properties or features whatsoever. That is, we're left with an idea of nothing, an idea with no content, a non-idea.

And it's exactly the same story for the would-be idea or concept of matter. Strip away from the idea of matter all of its mind-dependent properties or features (*i.e.*, *all* of its properties or features), and we're left with an idea of something that has no properties or features at all. The very idea of matter turns out to be an idea that's bereft of any content whatsoever – it's an empty idea, a non-idea, an idea we cannot in fact entertain, try as we might. In short, matter is *conceptually impossible* – we can't even *think* that there could be such a thing in existence, and once more people who claim that there is such a thing as matter quite literally have no idea what they are talking about.

Indeed with this last argument, Berkeley is putting the boot into the kind of would-be idea of a material object or of matter itself that (for instance) Locke alludes to when he says that our idea of any given substance includes, in addition to our ideas of its properties, some vague and altogether unclear idea of an underlying something whose properties these are (see above, pp. 43–4). As we've just seen, Berkeley strips away from this would-be idea the ideas we have of an object's properties or of matter's properties, and concludes that there's nothing left for us to have an idea about. Indeed it's amusing to see the wit with which he gives the resulting concept of matter a really good pummelling on these grounds, for example at §75 of the *Principles*, where he calls matter a 'stupid thoughtless *somewhat*'. (And as an aside, in §§74–5 we also find him claiming that by entertaining the belief that there is such a thing as matter, we risk cutting ourselves off from God. Berkeley's thinking here is that on the materialist's view it is matter which causes us to have the perceptual ideas that we do, and hence God has at best an *indirect* involvement in our everyday lives, as the creator of matter. On Berkeley's own account of course, God is intimately involved in every step of our everyday lives, as the *direct* cause of the perceptual ideas that we each have.)

Before we go on to consider some of the common objections to Berkeley's 'anti-abstractionist' strategies here, it's again worth emphasising another potentially puzzling feature of his attack on abstract ideas and the arguments he bases on it. Throughout the *Principles* and the *Dialogues* we find him claiming on the one hand that abstract ideas like the supposed idea of a mind-independent material object are *empty, devoid of content* or *meaningless*, and on the other hand that they are ideas of something which is *impossible, contradictory* or *repugnant*, and indeed on a mysterious third hand that it's *impossible, contradictory* or a *repugnancy* that we should be able to entertain such ideas. Again, which is it to be? Is it the case that we can entertain these abstract ideas or not? Is the problem that we can entertain them, but that they are ideas of something that's impossible and hence which can't possibly exist in reality? Or is the problem that we can't even entertain them? If it's the latter, is the reason why we can't entertain them that they are non-ideas (ideas of nothing, ideas that have no content), or that their content is contradictory nonsense? We'll return to these questions in a short while.

Two common objections to berkeley's attack on abstract ideas

Commentators have raised numerous objections to Berkeley's attack on abstract ideas and the arguments he goes on to base on it, and here I'm going to present two of the more common criticisms for you to consider. After I've done this, I'm going to argue that there's more to Berkeley's position here than perhaps first meets the eye, and that once we've taken on board the real driving force behind his arguments, they can in fact be provisionally defended against the two common objections in question – but only at a significant cost.

The first objection is that Berkeley's attack on abstract ideas can only work on an 'imagistic' account of the nature of ideas. According to this objection, Berkeley thinks that what we're doing when we're entertaining an idea is that we're forming a little image or picture in our mind's eye of whatever it is that the idea is of. Specifically, he thinks that ideas or concepts are all reducible to *perceptual* images – the things that we're aware of in the first instance when we perceive using our senses, or when we recall things we've perceived previously. In this way, Berkeley is accused of collapsing *conception* (the process by which we form ideas generally) into *perception* (the process by which we form mental images on the basis of what our senses tell us).

The objection continues that Berkeley's attack on abstract ideas can only succeed *if* this is what the process of forming ideas is in fact like. For example, it might well seem impossible for us to come up with a little *mental image* of an object's colour that's neither red, nor black, nor white, nor any other particular determinate colour. Or it might well seem impossible to come up with a little mental image of a material object that has no properties whatsoever. But surely there are good reasons to think that this *isn't* what the process of forming ideas is in fact like. It seems that we *can* entertain an idea of this, that or the other *without* having to conjure up a little mental picture of whatever it is that the idea is of. In which case, it's far less clear (if not downright false) that an idea of a material object, for instance, will be an empty one just because in entertaining the idea we're not thinking of (by picturing to ourselves) the particular size, colour and shape *etc.* that some material object or other happens to have. Despite the fact that all material objects *in reality* will have some particular determinate size, colour and shape *etc.*, can we not after all entertain the thought of a material object in general without having *in mind* the particular determinate size, colour and shape *etc.* that some material object or other happens to have?

Another common (and indeed related) objection to Berkeley's attack on abstract ideas is that he mistakenly thinks that a given idea must have the same features as whatever it is out there in the world that it's an idea of. For instance, he thinks that a triangle that exists in our thoughts must be either equilateral or right-angled or isosceles *etc.* because all triangles in reality are triangles of some particular determinate kind or other. Or he thinks that it's impossible for the property of extension to exist in isolation from all other properties in our thoughts because it's impossible that it should do so in reality.

In other words, Berkeley is accused of treating our ideas as if they were the things in the real world that they are ideas of, and consequently of thinking that the characterizations and logical rules that apply to things in the real word also apply to ideas. It is *real* triangles, not *ideas* of triangles (*i.e.*, the triangles 'in our heads') that are triangular, and that must be particular and determinate in nature. It is *real* material objects, not the *concept* of a material object (*i.e.*, a material object 'in our heads'), that must have a particular, determinate shape and size and so on. And it's the contents of the real world out there that can't defy the laws of logic, not the contents of our thoughts. (For instance, it's impossible that there should be a square circle in reality, but it's not impossible that there should be an idea of such a thing.) Once we bear this in mind, the objection goes, we'll see that we *can* entertain an idea of a material object that has no determinate features, and that we *can* conceive of extension in isolation from all other properties, and so forth.

Revisiting two puzzling features of Berkeley's attack on abstract ideas

We'll come back to these objections in a moment. Before we do though, I want to recall and resolve some apparently puzzling features of Berkeley's attack on abstract ideas. Specifically, we saw in the first place that Berkeley says on the one hand that what can't possibly be the case *in reality* can't possibly be the case *in our thoughts*, and on the other hand that what we can't possibly conceive of *in our thoughts* can't possibly be the case *in reality*, and we asked which of these it is to be. And in the second place, we saw him saying that abstract ideas (such as the idea of a mind-independent material object) are *empty, devoid of content* or *meaningless*, **and** that they are ideas of something which is *impossible, contradictory* or *repugnant*, **and** that it's *impossible, contradictory* or *repugnant* that we should have such an idea. Again we asked which of these it is to be.

Berkeley's genuine answer, which he means in all seriousness, is that it's to be all of these things, and the key to understanding why this should be the case lies in an appreciation of what's *really* driving his attack on abstract ideas and the arguments he goes on to base on it, namely his '*esse* is *percipi*' thesis – his claim that for everyday objects and their properties, their existence consists in the fact that they are being perceived. I should note though that it's controversial for me to state that this is the case, because some Berkeley scholars don't think that there's any link whatsoever between his attack on abstract ideas and his '*esse* is *percipi*' thesis. However I think that there's ample evidence in both the *Principles* and the *Dialogues* that Berkeley takes his attack on abstract ideas to *proceed from* his starting claim that everyday objects and their properties are ideas (and specifically, sensations), and hence whose *esse* is *percipi*. (I should also acknowledge that in reaching this view I was inspired by Martha Brandt Bolton's article 'Berkeley's Objection to Abstract Ideas and Unconceived Objects'.)

Recall that Berkeley states that everyday objects and their properties are identical with ideas right at the start of Part I the *Principles* (at §§1–8), and also in the first meaningful exchange in the *Dialogues* (after Hylas has expressed astonishment at Philonous' immaterialism and after they've agreed on the definition of scepticism). That this should be the very first thing that Berkeley attends to in both of his major works on metaphysics is, I believe, no coincidence. (Remember that although the Introduction to the *Principles* precedes §§1–8 of Part I, it was conceived as an introduction to all of the intended Parts of the *Principles*, including those parts that Berkeley planned to write on topics other than metaphysics.) I think that he brings in the identification of everyday objects and their properties with ideas straight away because this is what is going to fuel many of the arguments he goes on to provide us with.

Moreover, there are a number of passages in the texts in which Berkeley either strongly implies or explicit states that the '*esse* is *percipi*' thesis is the *reason why* the very idea of an everyday object and/or its properties, or indeed matter, existing beyond the mind should be rejected as either meaningless and/or a contradiction in terms. To give a couple of examples, at §6 of Part I of the *Principles*, having provided his '*esse* is *percipi*' thesis as a premise, Berkeley concludes that it is 'unintelligible and involving all the absurdity of abstraction' to claim that everyday objects exist beyond the mind. And at pp. 232–3 of the *Dialogues*, Philonous dismisses the claim that matter exists beyond the mind now as meaningless, and now as contradictory, citing as a premise the fact it's 'repugnant' that 'ideas should exist in what doth not perceive'. Indeed in numerous other places, Berkeley uses the very same language in his rejection of abstract ideas – rejecting them now as empty, meaningless, contradictory, impossible *etc.* – as he does in dismissing the claim that either ideas, everyday objects, their properties or matter might exist beyond the mind. All in all, we can see from these passages that Berkeley often presents as a premise the '*esse* is *percipi*' thesis, or more specifically his claim that everyday objects and their properties are (collections of) sensations, before concluding directly that everyday objects and their properties can't be abstracted from existence in the mind, either in thought or in reality.

If this interpretation is right, then Berkeley's principle reason for thinking that we can't frame abstract ideas, including the idea of an everyday object and its properties existing beyond the mind, is that everyday objects and their properties are (collections of) ideas (and more specifically, sensations). Consequently, we can appreciate now why Berkeley says alternatively that abstract ideas are *empty*, *devoid of content* or *meaningless*, that they are ideas of something that's *impossible*, *contradictory* or *repugnant*, or even that it is *impossible*, *contradictory* or *repugnant* that we should have such ideas.

Let's focus on the example of an everyday object existing beyond the mind. For Berkeley, it's *impossible*, *repugnant*, *absurd* and a *contradiction in terms* that there should be such a thing – everyday objects are identical with collections of sensations, and it's impossible for sensations to exist beyond the mind. And for exactly the same reason, the very idea of an everyday object existing beyond the mind is an idea of something that's a *contradiction in terms* – in trying to frame such an idea you're trying to think of something that can't possibly exist beyond the mind (namely, a collection of sensations) existing beyond the mind.

What's more, it follows from the claim that everyday objects are collections of sensations that the very idea of an everyday object existing beyond the mind is an *empty* idea, a *non-idea*, an idea of *nothing*. Strip away from the would-be idea of a mind-independent everyday object all of the features of an everyday object that depend for their existence on being perceived by the mind (namely, all of the ideas or sensations that make it up), and you're suddenly left with an idea with no content – there's nothing left for you to think about, or to have an idea *of*. So there can be *no such idea*. It's quite literally *inconceivable* that there should be an everyday object existing beyond the mind – it's *unthinkable* that there should be, and we can't even frame the idea that there is. Put another way, it's *impossible* or a *contradiction in terms* that there should be such an idea – we'd be trying to frame an idea that has no content, which we simply cannot do.

And finally, the very claim that there is such a thing as an everyday object existing beyond the mind is *meaningless* – the supposed idea at the heart of this claim turns out to be devoid of content, an empty idea, and so the claim itself turns out to be *unintelligible*, *incomprehensible* or *mere jargon*, as Berkeley sometimes says. When someone claims that there is such a thing as an everyday object existing beyond the mind, they don't convey any meaningful idea at all – they're talking nonsense.

So too, we're now in a better position to see why Berkeley says, at least with respect to everyday objects and their properties, that what can't possibly be the case *in reality* can't possibly be the case *in our thoughts*, **and** that what can't possibly be the case *in our thoughts* can't possibly be the case *in reality*. (And here, I should acknowledge my debt to Kenneth P. Winkler's book *Berkeley: An Interpretation* for getting me thinking in the first place that Berkeley believed both that what is impossible is inconceivable and *vice versa*.) We saw above how Berkeley argued that we can't frame an idea whose content features the property of extension in isolation from all other properties *because* what can't possibly be the case in reality can't possibly be the case in our thoughts. For him, the property of extension is a feature or function of the ideas or sensations in our minds – specifically, he thinks that the property of extension that an object has is simply the expanse of the sensations of colour that we perceive when we look at it, or the expanse of tactual sensations (or 'feels') that we perceive when we run our hands over it. On this account, extension can't possibly exist in isolation from other properties like the colour or the 'feel' of a given object. And consequently, neither can we entertain the idea that it does – to think of the property of extension is to think of the expanse of colours or the expanse of 'feels' that it is.

Likewise, in the *Dialogues* version of the Argument from Conceptual Inseparability, we found Philonous arguing that *because* it's impossible to frame an idea of the property of extension in isolation from 'all other sensible qualities', it's necessarily the case that the property of extension can't exist independent of 'all other sensible qualities' in reality. Again if we bear in mind that Berkeley holds that the property of extension is a feature or function of the sensations in our minds, and specifically that extension is either an expanse of colour sensations or an expanse of tactual sensations (or 'feels'), we can see why Philonous says this. We can't frame an idea of the property of extension in isolation from 'all other sensible qualities' because to think of the property of extension is to think of an expanse of colours or of 'feels', and consequently the property of extension can't exist in isolation from 'all other sensible qualities' in reality because the property of extension *is* an expanse of colour or an expanse of 'feels'.

In short, *given* Berkeley's starting claim that everyday objects and their properties are (collections of) sensations in our minds, we can see that with respect to the objects out there in the world and their properties, existence in reality and existence in our thoughts *coincide*. No wonder then that what can't possibly exist in reality can't possibly exist in our thoughts and *vice versa*, and that it's the case that the very idea of an everyday object, its properties or even matter existing beyond the mind is simultaneously an empty idea, an idea we can't even entertain, and the idea of something that's impossible.

And as an aside here, we can now see why it's ultimately irrelevant whether or not Berkeley misinterpreted Locke's account of the nature of Secondary Qualities (see above, pp. 49–50). For Berkeley, the properties of everyday objects, including what others call the 'Secondary Qualities', *are* sensations in us – they *aren't* features of mind-independent material objects out there, such as the dispositions that material objects might have to cause the sensations we experience when we perceive that an object is red or sweet or noisy *etc*. If the colour red (for instance) is a sensation in our minds and we eliminate any mention of this sensation from the would-be idea of the mind-independent property of the colour red then there's *nothing* left for this supposed idea to be an idea *of*. Whether or not Berkeley correctly identified that *Locke* defined Secondary Qualities like colour as the dispositional properties that material objects really do have is by the by. *Berkeley* defined them as sensations in our minds, and that's all he needs for his argument that the very idea of a mind-independent property is an empty idea and/or a contradiction in terms.

Common objections to Berkeley's attack on abstract ideas revisited

If it's true that Berkeley's attack on abstract ideas and the arguments he goes on to base on it are fuelled by his prior claim that everyday objects and their properties are (collections of) sensations, we are also in a position to provisionally defend him against the common objections that we saw earlier.

The first objection was that Berkeley's arguments can only work on an 'imagistic' account of the nature of ideas. The complaint here was that Berkeley mistakenly thinks that what we're doing when we're entertaining an idea is that we're forming a little image or picture in our mind's eye of whatever it is that the idea is of, and that his attack on abstract ideas can only succeed if this what the process of forming ideas is like. Even if it were the case that we can't form a *mental image* of an object's colour that's neither red, nor black, nor white, nor any other particular determinate colour, or that it's impossible for us to come up with a *mental image* of a material object that has no properties whatsoever, is it not possible for us to have, say, *intellectual notions* of such things?

As we saw back in Chapter 3 though Berkeley himself doesn't think that *all* of the thoughts in our heads are little mental images (see above, pp. 57 & 106). He tells us that 'strictly speaking' we can only have ideas of things that we can perceive, and indeed he does speak in terms of the things that we perceive being akin to little images in our mind's eye. However, he very occasionally uses the term 'idea' in a 'wide sense' to cover not just the mental images we're given in perception, but also thoughts or 'notions' of unperceivable entities such as God and other people's minds. And tellingly he extends his attack on abstract ideas to these non-imagistic thoughts or notions as well (see, *e.g.*, pp. 232–3 of the *Dialogues*).

So what of the proposed intellectual notion of an everyday object existing beyond the mind, for example? Well, given the premise that everyday objects are collections of sensations, there can be no such intellectual notion. As we've seen, it would follow that the very thought that an everyday object exists beyond the mind is a contradiction in terms and an empty idea that's devoid of content. And this is the case *however* we happen to try to capture that thought – whether via a little image in our mind's eye, via a non-imagistic intellectual notion or via any other means. So the complaint that Berkeley's arguments here can only work on an 'imagistic' account of the nature of ideas turns out to be unfounded.

The other objection was that Berkeley mistakenly thinks that a given idea must have the same features as whatever it is out there in the world that it's an idea of – that the characterizations and logical rules that apply to things in the real world also apply to ideas. But once we take on board Berkeley's starting assertion that everyday objects and their properties are *identical* with ideas an interesting consequence emerges. (Again I'm indebted to Martha Brandt Bolton's article 'Berkeley's Objection to Abstract Ideas and Unconceived Objects' for this line of thought.) Since objects and their properties are identical with our ideas, a triangle out there in the world is one and the same thing as a triangle in our heads. This being the case, if a given triangle out there in the world is a particular determinate kind of triangle (as it must be) then the same is true of the triangle in our heads with which it is identical. (What's in play here is one of the basic rules of philosophy known as the 'law of the indiscernibility of identicals', according to which two things that are identical will have exactly the same properties and features as one another, by definition). Likewise, if it's impossible for the property of extension to exist in isolation from all other properties in *reality* then it's impossible for it to do so in our *thoughts*, precisely because reality and the contents of our thoughts *coincide*. In short, if it's true that objects and their properties are (collections of) ideas, Berkeley is quite right to think that the ideas in our minds which make up the everyday objects that populate the real world have the same properties as, and are subject to the same laws of logic as, the objects with which they're identical.

This is why, for example, Berkeley states at §5 of Part I of the *Principles* that we can only conceive separately (*i.e.*, think of separately) those things that can either exist separately from one another in reality, or that we can perceive separately from one another using our senses. The everyday objects and their properties that exist in reality and that we perceive to exist in reality are (collections of) sensations – these objects as they are in (our perceptual experience of) reality and as they are in our thoughts are one and the same thing. It's because they are identical in this way that what's true of the former must simultaneously be true of the latter.

However, even if Berkeley's prior identification of everyday objects and their properties with sensations allows us to defend his attack on abstract ideas against at least some of the criticisms that have been directed at it, it does so at a considerable cost. (And in fact various Berkeley scholars make the kind of point that I'm about to run past you.) Wasn't it the case that Berkeley introduced his attack on abstract ideas to *establish* or *demonstrate* that everyday objects and their properties can't possibly exist beyond the mind? If so, then since his attack on abstract ideas and the arguments he bases on it *proceed* from the starting premise that everyday objects and their properties are (collections of) sensations and as such can't possibly exist beyond the mind, he is simply arguing in a circle. In effect, he'd be trying to prove that everyday objects and their properties can't possibly exist beyond the mind by appealing to the premise that everyday objects and their properties can't possibly exist beyond the mind. His attack on abstract ideas and the arguments he bases on it won't convince anyone who doesn't already accept that everyday objects and their properties are (collections of) sensations.

vi. CONCLUSION – WHERE THIS LEAVES US

This obviously invites the question 'is it *true* that everyday objects and their properties are (collections of) sensations?', and in summarizing what we've seen of his various arguments for immaterialism and idealism it becomes clear that he's failed to give us any *good* reasons for thinking that the answer to this question is 'yes'. Recall that in §§1–8 of Part I of the *Principles*, and early on in the *Dialogues*, Berkeley simply *asserted* that the things we perceive using our senses, including everyday objects and their properties, are (collections) of sensations. We were given no independent *justification* at that point for thinking that this is in fact true. However, he then proceeded to provide us with two arguments that were intended to *prove* that the properties of everyday objects are nothing other than sensations – the Identity Argument and the Argument from Perceptual Relativity. But I argued earlier in this chapter that the Identity Argument *fails* to establish that properties like heat and cold, taste and smell are identical with sensations, and we saw that the Argument from Perceptual Relativity itself *proceeds* from the very claim it's attempting to establish, and thus is itself circular. The Master Argument meanwhile turns out to be at best a reiteration of an early argument in which Berkeley jumps from the starting claim that everyday objects and their properties are (collections of) sensations to the conclusion that they can't possibly exist beyond the mind. As such the Master Argument does nothing by way of convincing us that this starting claim itself is true. And now it turns out that Berkeley's attack on abstract ideas and the arguments he bases on it themselves *rely* on the same starting claim, and in doing so leave unresolved the question of whether it's *true* that everyday objects and their properties are (collections of) sensations which can't exist beyond the mind.

In short, on my (admittedly controversial) interpretation of what he's up to, Berkeley has *failed* to give us any decent, non-circular arguments for the conclusion that everyday objects and their properties are (collections of) sensations and as such cannot possibly exist beyond the mind. It's this conclusion that's at the heart of his arguments for immaterialism and idealism, but it turns out that he doesn't give us any *good* reason for thinking that it's true.

So where does this leave us? Well, even if Berkeley fails to *prove* that there's no such thing as matter and that everyday objects and their properties are (collections of) sensations that can't possibly exist beyond the mind, it doesn't necessarily follow that he's *wrong* about this. There are many things in life that we can't *prove*, but that we take to be *true* nonetheless. In which case we can still ask whether his philosophical account is the kind of thing we might be prepared to accept anyway, even in the absence of a decent supporting argument. Addressing this question of course was the business of Chapter 3 above. Central to Berkeley's system meanwhile, as we've seen, is the crucial claim that all we are aware of when we perceive using our senses are sensations. Some people think that if he's right about this, then immaterialism and idealism inevitably follow. (For instance, this was the view of one of Berkeley's fiercest early critics, the eighteenth-century Scottish philosopher Thomas Reid). Be that as it may, deciding whether or not *you* think that Berkeley's right when he tells us that all we perceive are sensations is one of your principle tasks as a student of his philosophy. If your view is different from Berkeley's, don't just assume that you're right. Can you prove that you're right and he's wrong? That's your challenge.

THE STANDARD EDITIONS OF
BERKELEY'S WORKS

Berkeley scholars today standardly use A. A. Luce and T. E. Jessop's nine-volume edition of Berkeley's complete works.

- Luce, A. A. & Jessop T. E. (eds), *The Works of George Berkeley Bishop of Cloyne*, 9 volumes. (London: Thomas Nelson and Sons Ltd, 1948–1957.)

If you have access to this edition of his complete works (for instance in a university library), you'll find *A Treatise Concerning the Principles of Human Knowledge* ('the *Principles*') and *Three Dialogues between Hylas and Philonous* ('the *Dialogues*') in Volume 2. Berkeley's other writings that I mention in Chapter 1 are located in various other volumes, as follows:

- *An Essay Towards a New Theory of Vision* – Volume 1
- *The Theory of Vision . . . Vindicated and Explained* – Volume 1
- *The Philosophical Commentaries* – Volume 1
- *De Motu* – Volume 4
- *Alciphron* – Volume 3
- *The Analyst* – Volume 4
- *The Querist* – Volume 6
- *Siris* – Volume 5

The Luce and Jessop editions of the *Principles* and the *Dialogues* have been republished in a student-friendly form in two volumes edited by Jonathan Dancy, each with a useful and substantial editor's introduction to the work in question:

*   Berkeley, George, *A Treatise Concerning the Principles of Human Knowledge*, Dancy, Jonathan (ed.). (OUP: Oxford, 1998)
*   Berkeley, George, *Three Dialogues between Hylas and Philonous*, Dancy, Jonathan (ed.). (OUP: Oxford, 1998)

There are also many other editions of both the *Principles* and the *Dialogues* currently in print. Every edition of the *Principles* follows Berkeley's division of that work into numbered sections. In *Starting with Berkeley* I have used the symbol '§' to stand for 'section' (and '§§' for 'sections') when I have provided references to portions of the text of the *Principles*. References such as '*Principles* §5' indicate sections in 'Part I' of the *Principles*, rather than sections in the 'Introduction to the *Principles*'. I have made it clear when I am referring to sections in the Introduction to the *Principles*.

The *Dialogues* isn't divided into numbered sections (although it is divided into the three dialogues mentioned in the full title). When I have provided references to portions of the text of the *Dialogues*, I have done so by page number. The page numbers I use are those in the Luce and Jessop edition of the *Dialogues*, and these typically differ from the page numbers used in other editions. Dancy however makes it clear which pages in his edition of the *Dialogues* are equivalent to the original pages in the Luce and Jessop edition, so you shouldn't have any problems locating the page references that I have used if you have the Dancy edition. If you have neither the Luce and Jessop edition nor the Dancy edition of the *Dialogues*, you will face a trickier task locating my page references. To give you some guidance in this case, bear in mind that the 'First Dialogue' takes up pp. 171–207 in the Luce and Jessop edition, and the 'Second Dialogue' and the 'Third Dialogue' take up pp. 208–26 and 227–63 respectively.

BIBLIOGRAPHY AND RECOMMENDED FURTHER READING

Some good general commentaries on Berkeley:

- Dancy, Jonathan, *Berkeley: An Introduction* (Oxford: Basil Blackwell, 1987)
- Pitcher, George, *Berkeley* (London: Routledge & Kegan Paul, 1977)
- Tipton, I.C., *Berkeley: The Philosophy of Immaterialism* (London: Methuen, 1974)
- Warnock, G.J., *Berkeley* (3rd ed.) (Oxford: Basil Blackwell, 1982)
- Winkler, Kenneth P., *Berkeley: An Interpretation* (Oxford: Clarendon Press, 1989)

A good commentary on the Principles:

- Fogelin, Robert J., *Routledge Philosophy Guidebook to Berkeley and the Principles of Human Knowledge* (London: Routledge, 2001)

A couple of good commentaries on the Dialogues:

- Garrett, Aaron, *Berkeley's Three Dialogues: A Reader's Guide* (London: Continuum, 2008)
- Stoneham, Tom, *Berkeley's World: An Examination of the Three Dialogues* (Oxford: OUP, 2002)

BIBLIOGRAPHY

An edited collection containing some good essays on various aspects of Berkeley's philosophy:

* Martin, C.B. & Armstrong, D.M. (eds), *Locke and Berkeley: A Collection of Critical Essays* (London: Macmillan, 1968)

A couple of good internet resources on Berkeley:

* *Stanford Encyclopedia of Philosophy* – entry on George Berkeley: http://plato.stanford.edu/entries/berkeley/
* *The Internet Encyclopedia of Philosophy* – entry on George Berkeley: http://www.iep.utm.edu/b/berkeley.htm

Other publications that I've mentioned:

* Bolton, Martha Brandt, 'Berkeley's Objection to Abstract Ideas and Unconceived Objects', in Sosa, Ernest (ed.) *Essays on the Philosophy of George Berkeley* (Dordrecht: D. Reidel, 1987)
* Descartes, René, 'Meditations', in Descartes, René (ed.), *Meditations and Other Metaphysical Writings*, Clarke, Desmond M. (tr. & ed.), (London: Penguin, 1998)
* Hume, David, 'An Enquiry Concerning Human Understanding', in Hume, David, *Enquiries Concerning Human Understanding and Concerning the Principles of Morals* (3rd edition), Niddith, P.H. (ed.) (Oxford: OUP, 1975)
* Locke, John, *An Essay Concerning Human Understanding*, Nidditch, Peter H. (ed.) (New York: OUP, 1975).
* Malebranche, Nicolas, *The Search after Truth*, Lennon, Thomas M. & Olscamp, Paul J. (trs. & eds.) (Cambridge: CUP, 1997)